PLANNING CONTROL –
DEVELOPMENT, PERMISSION
AND ENFORCEMENT

Richard E Smith

Acknowledgements

Crown copyright material is reproduced with the permission of the controller of HMSO and the Queen's Printer for Scotland.

Please note: References to the masculine include, where appropriate, the feminine.

Published by RICS Business Services Limited

a wholly owned subsidiary of

The Royal Institution of Chartered Surveyors

under the RICS Books imprint

Surveyor Court

Westwood Business Park

Coventry CV4 8JE

UK

www.ricsbooks.com

No responsibility for loss or damage caused to any person acting or refraining from action as a result of the material included in this publication can be accepted by the author, publisher or RICS.

ISBN 978 1 84219 289 2

ISBN 1 84219 289 2 (prior to January 2007)

Typeset in Great Britain by Columns Design Ltd, Reading, Berks

Printed in Great Britain by Bell & Bain, Glasgow

Contents

Contents

Contents

Contents

Contents

Preface

While chartered surveyors do not normally need the *breadth* of understanding of the law of their opposite numbers in the legal profession, in a number of key areas of application to construction and property they need a similar *depth* of legal knowledge. Exactly what the key areas may be depends to some extent on the nature of the surveyor's practice. An obvious example is the law relating to planning. There are certainly specialist surveyors who, apart from the procedural aspects of applications for planning permission, would actually know more about the case law on development control than the average lawyer in general practice.

So surveyors need law and, for a variety of reasons, need to maintain and develop their understanding of it. Changing trends or individual variations in clients' requirements mean that from time to time even the best practitioners (perhaps especially the best practitioners) will feel the need to expand their knowledge. The knowledge acquired at college or in studying for the Assessment of Professional Competence (APC) has a limited shelf life and needs to be constantly updated to maintain its currency. Even specialists working in their areas of expertise need a source of reference as an aide-mémoire or as a first port of call in more detailed research.

The Case in Point series

RICS Books is committed to meeting the needs of surveying and other professionals and the Case in Point series typifies that commitment. It is aimed at those who need to upgrade their legal knowledge, or update it, or have access to a good first reference point at the outset of an inquiry. A particular difficulty is the burgeoning of reported decisions of the courts. The sheer scale of the law reports, both general and specialist, makes it very hard even to be aware of recent trends, let alone identify the significance of a particular decision. Thus it was decided to focus on developments in case law. In any given matter, the practitioner will want to be directed efficiently and painlessly to the decision that bears upon the matter he or she is dealing with, in other words to 'the case in point'.

The books in the Case in Point series offer a wealth of legal information which is essential in its practical application to the surveyor's work. Authors have been chosen as having the ability to be selective and succinct, thus achieving a high degree of relevance without sacrificing accessibility. The series has developed as a collection of specialist handbooks which can deliver what practitioners need – the law on the matter they are handling, when they want it.

Planning control: development, permission and enforcement – Richard Smith

Despite various reforms and attempts at modernisation, the most recent of which was the *Planning and Compulsory Purchase Act* 2004, the planning system is still recognisably that which was set up in 1948. So the structure itself of local planning authorities development plans and the development control and enforcement mechanisms is statutory.

But while a knowledge of the structure is necessary, it is by no means enough for an understanding of how the system actually works. For in the hands of local planning authorities and the inspectors of the Secretary of State is decision-making power. How that power is exercised and in 'crunch' cases is reviewed by the courts is what actually defines and describes the operation of the planning system. The case law is the flesh and blood which makes the statutory skeleton recognisable and gives it life. Thus section 55(2)(d) of the principal act (the *Town and Country Planning Act* 1990) merely states that there will be no development involved in 'the use of any buildings or other land within the curtilage of a dwellinghouse for any purpose incidental to the enjoyment of the dwellinghouse as such'. It took the Court of Appeal in *Wallington v Secretary of State for Wales* to decide that this meant that the keeping of 40 dogs in a house constituted development, entitling the planning authority to serve an enforcement notice. Of course, few of the cases deal with such quaint examples. Crucial in commercial development are cases on the effect of planning agreements such as *Tesco Stores v Secretary of State for Environment* or on judicial review of permission for a major retail centre redevelopment, as in *R (on the application of Ghadami) v Harlow DC* last year.

Whether residential or commercial interests are involved, the need for planning permission and the enforcement of control of breaches are at the heart of the development system. A major tool in assessing and advising on the prospects for success or challenge in applications, objections, appeals and enforcement proceedings is a collection of the case law on these subjects.

Richard Smith is admirably qualified for the task of compiling the collection and providing the commentary. Formerly a practising solicitor, he now teaches law on surveying courses at Sheffield Hallam University, where he is Principal Lecturer and Course Director of the MSc in Property Appraisal and Management. Already author of the successful *Estate Agency* title in the Case in Point series, Richard's academic work and especially his contributions to RICS CPD events give him insights into the practical needs of surveyors and the skills to meet those needs.

Anthony Lavers, 2006.
Professional Support Lawyer, White & Case, London.
Visiting Professor of Law, Oxford Brookes University, Oxford.
Consultant Editor, Case in Point series.

List of Acts, Statutory Instruments and abbreviations

The following Acts and Statutory Instruments are referred to in this publication.

Where an Act or Statutory Instrument is mentioned frequently, it is referred to by the abbreviation in brackets that follows.

The primary act in this book is the *Town and Country Planning Act* 1990 (**'the 1990 Act'**). Where section numbers are used they are taken from the 1990 Act unless otherwise stated.

Acquisition of Land Act 1981

Agricultural Holdings Act 1986

Caravan Sites and Control of Development Act 1960

Criminal Justice Act 2003

Greater London (General Powers) Act 1973

Highways Act 1980

Housing Act 1957

Housing Act 1985

Human Rights Act 1998

Landlord and Tenant Act 1954

Local Government Act 1972

Planning and Compensation Act 1991

Planning and Compulsory Purchase Act 2004

Rent Act 1977

Summer Time Act 1972

Town and Country Planning Act 1957

Town and Country Planning Act 1971

Town and Country Planning Act 1990 (**'the 1990 Act'**)

Town and Country Planning (Control of Advertisements) Regulations 1992 (SI 1992/666)

Town and Country Planning (Enforcement Notices and Appeals) (England) Regulations 2002 (SI 2002/2682)

Town and Country Planning (Enforcement Notices and Appeals) (Wales) Regulations 2003 (SI 2003/394)

Town and Country Planning (Environmental Impact Assessment) (England and Wales) Regulations 1999 (SI 1999/293)

Town and Country Planning General Development Order 1963 (SI 1963/709) (**'GDO 1963'**)

Town and Country Planning General Development Order 1977 (SI 1977/289) (**'GDO 1977'**)

Town and Country Planning General Development Order 1988 (SI 1988/1813)

Town and Country Planning (General Development Procedure) Order 1995 (SI 1995/419)

Town and Country Planning (General Permitted Development) Order 1995 (SI 1995/418) (**'GPDO'**)

Town and Country Planning (Inquiries Procedure) (England) Rules 2000 (SI 2000/1624)

Town and Country Planning (Inquiries Procedure) (Wales) Rules 2003 (SI 2003/1266)

Town and Country Planning (Minerals) Regulations 1995 (SI 1995/2863)

Town and Country Planning (Temporary Stop Notice) (England) Regulations 2005 (SI 2005/206)

Town and Country Planning (Use Classes) Order 1950 (SI 1950/1131)

Town and Country Planning (Use Classes) Order 1963 (SI 1963/708)

Town and Country Planning (Use Classes) Order 1972 (SI 1972/1385)

Town and Country Planning (Use Classes) Order 1987 (SI 1987/764)

European Convention on Human Rights and Fundamental Freedoms

Relevance to Scotland
The system of planning control in Scotland is substantially the same as in England and Wales. The *Town and Country Planning (Scotland) Act* 1997 contains the same definition of development and the same planning permission and enforcement regime as the *Town and Country Planning Act* 1990. The organisation of the statutes is different (for example, the definition of development is in section 55 of the English Act and section 26 of the Scottish Act)

and occasionally different terms are used (e.g. interdict instead of injunction) to reflect differences in Scots law, but the outcome is largely the same. So the book provides cases of direct relevance to Scottish planning law, although obviously the statutory references are different. In fact, some Scottish cases are included (e.g. the Grampian case which established the so-called 'Grampian' planning condition used throughout the UK) because the Scottish courts are examining provisions which are identical to the English provisions. Scottish cases are cited in English courts and vice versa. There are differences in the Scottish *Use Classes Order* and *General Permitted Development Order* (e.g. there is a different system of categorising use classes) but much of the content is very similar. In any event, the book does not purport to be a guide to the legislation. Its purpose is to set out key planning case law. In this it will prove useful to the Scottish practitioner.

The text of this publication is divided into commentary and case summaries. The commentary is enclosed between grey highlighted lines for ease of reference.

Table of cases

1
Development

Section 57 of the *Town and Country Planning Act* 1990 ('the 1990 Act') requires planning permission for the carrying out of any development on land. It is therefore crucial to know what the word 'development' encompasses. It is defined in the 1990 Act but the case law illuminates this definition.

1.1 MEANING OF DEVELOPMENT

Section 55 of the 1990 Act states that development means:

> 'the carrying out of building, engineering, mining or other operations in, on, over or under land, or the making of any material change in the use of any buildings or other land.'

It should be noted that whether something falls within the definition of development is largely a question of fact and degree and not of law. The courts have been reluctant to lay down general rules – each case should be decided on its own merits. See, for example, the judgment of the House of Lords in *Coleshill and District Investment Co v Minister of Housing and Local Government* (1969) below.

The definition in section 55 creates two principal kinds of development: operations and material change of use.

1.2 DISTINCTION BETWEEN OPERATIONS AND USE

Operations

The term 'operations' is usually taken to mean something that changes the physical character of land.

Cheshire County Council v Woodward (1962)

> '... having regard to the prepositions describing the operations as "in, on, over or under land", the concept ...

must be whether the physical character of the land has been changed by operations in or on it, secondly whether the physical character of what is under the land have been changed, for example by mining operations under the land, and, thirdly, whether the physical characteristics of the air above the land have been changed by operations ... over the land.' (Lord Parker CJ)

Use

Section 336 of the 1990 Act negatively defines use in relation to land as follows:

'"use", in relation to land, does not include the use of land for the carrying out of any building or other operations on it.'

This definition and the related meaning of 'operations' were examined in *Parkes v Secretary of State for the Environment.*

Parkes v Secretary of State for the Environment (1979)

The Court of Appeal held that the storing, sorting and processing of scrap was a use, not an operation. Lord Denning MR categorised the word 'operations' in the 1990 Act as comprising activities which result in some physical alteration to the land which has some degree of permanence, whereas use comprises activities which are done in, alongside or on the land but do not interfere with the actual physical characteristics of the land.

1.3   BUILDING OPERATIONS

Building operations is defined in section 55 as including:

- demolition of buildings;
- rebuilding;
- structural alterations of or additions to buildings; and
- other operations normally undertaken by a person carrying on business as a builder.

Building is defined in section 336 as including:

'any structure or erection, and any part of a building, as so defined, but does not include plant or machinery comprised in a building.'

Erection, in relation to buildings, is defined as including extension, alteration and re-erection.

The meaning of building was considered in *Barvis v Secretary of State for the Environment*. The now standard 'three-fold test' of size, degree of permanence, and physical attachment was adopted by way of analogy with rating law.

Barvis v Secretary of State for the Environment (1971)

B erected a mobile tower crane at a depot. It was 89 feet high and ran on a steel track fixed in concrete. B claimed that it was not part of the 'realty' as it was intended that the crane be moved on and off the land when required.

Mr Justice Bridge thought it was wrong to substitute issues of real property law and cases on fixtures for the statutory definition in the 1990 Act. Instead he found assistance from a case on the meaning of building or structure for the purposes of rating (*Cardiff Rating Authority v Guest Keen Baldwin's Iron and Steel Co* (1949)). The judge in that case picked out three factors which, whilst not conclusive, would indicate that something was in the nature of a building or structure. These are:

- substantial size – such that it has or would normally be constructed on the land and not ready made;
- some degree of permanence – so it would normally remain in place and only be removed by pulling down or taking to pieces; and
- physical attachment, although the fact that something is not so attached is not conclusive.

The judge also observed that a limited degree of motion does not necessarily prevent something from being in the nature of a structure.

> 'If, as a matter of impression, one looks objectively at this enormous crane, it seems to me impossible to say that it did not amount to a structure or erection.'

Something may be a building although it is not incorporated in the realty.

R v Swansea City Council, ex parte Elitestone Ltd (1993)

The appellants owned land on which 27 wooden self-built chalet-type dwellings had been erected by licence. They remained in the ownership of the licensees and so were not part of the realty.

Lord Justice Mann said that it was 'obvious' that the chalets were buildings. Incorporation into the realty is but one factor and not determinant either way. Having regard to the degree of permanence of the chalets and the effect on the physical quality of the land, it was common sense that the chalets were buildings for the purposes of planning law.

Permanent does not mean everlasting. It is a question of whether the degree of permanence is significant in the planning context.

Skerritts of Nottingham Ltd v Secretary of State for the Environment, Transport and the Regions (No. 2) (2000)

Each year an hotelier erected a marquee on the hotel lawn for a period of eight months. The marquee was 40 metres long, 17 metres wide, and 5 metres high.

The hotelier claimed that the marquee was not a building, as it did not satisfy the *Barvis* test of permanence.

The Court of Appeal held that permanence does not necessarily mean that the item must be on site for 365 days a year, otherwise its removal for a short time would avoid planning control. Permanence means a sufficient length of time to be of significance in the planning context. In the circumstances the planning inspector had been entitled to conclude that the marquee was a building.

1.3.1 Building operations excluded from the definition of development – section 55(2)(a)

Works of maintenance, improvement or alteration only affecting the interior

This exclusion is now subject to section 55(2A) (inserted by the *Planning and Compulsory Purchase Act* 2004) which allows the Secretary of State, by development order, to specify that interior works which increase the gross floorspace by a certain percentage are to be treated as development.

A planning condition can be used to restrict the use of floorspace created by internal works. See *Northampton Borough Council v First Secretary of State* (2005).

Works of maintenance, improvement or alteration that do not materially affect the external appearance of the building

It is external appearance that matters, not merely the exterior. Factors to be taken into account include visibility, the nature of the works and the nature of the building.

Burroughs Day v Bristol City Council (1996)

The appellant proposed alterations to a listed Georgian building involving the construction of a lift shaft with a flat roof. This would be situated in the valley gutter between the double ridges of a roof. It would not exceed the height of the ridges and would not be visible from the street.

The High Court judge held that the proposals were not interior works as they would alter the exterior surface of the roof. He also held that, as the 'external appearance' must be affected, not just the exterior, it must affect the way in which the exterior is seen. The effect must be judged for its materiality in relation to the building as a whole. Whether the effect on appearance is 'material' depends in part on the degree of visibility. It also depends on the nature of the building and the nature of the alteration.

The judge took account of the fact the building was listed, of some distinction and within a conservation area, but found that the works would not materially affect the external appearance of the building as they were invisible except from some unusual vantage points.

Something which affects the external appearance of a building but is not an operation cannot be development.

Kensington and Chelsea Royal London Borough Council v C G Hotels (1981)

The owners of a hotel installed floodlights without planning permission. A planning inspector held that no development

5

had occurred as the floodlights themselves were virtually invisible from the street and so did not materially affect the external appearance of the building. The planning authority appealed on the ground that at night the whole purpose of the floodlights was to affect the external appearance of the building. The Divisional Court held that the running of electricity through the apparatus was what materially affected the building's appearance. Since this was not an operation it could be not be development.

Distinction between improvement and rebuilding

There have been a number of cases where property owners have carried out substantial works but have claimed that no development has taken place because the works fall within section 55(2) (or its predecessors) as works of maintenance, alteration or improvements. It is a matter of fact and degree whether the works are such or are, in reality, rebuilding. Building operations are defined as including rebuilding.

Street v Essex County Council (1965)

Mr Street's bungalow was the subject of a demolition order because of its poor condition. He decided to repair the building, but found it necessary to demolish it down to the damp course, with the exception of two partition walls, and rebuild it.

In answer to an enforcement notice, Street claimed that he was carrying out works of maintenance. It was held that whether the works were maintenance or reconstruction was a matter of fact and degree. In the circumstances, the Minister was entitled to hold as a matter of fact that what took place was reconstruction.

It should be noted that if a building is so seriously damaged by fire that its reinstatement is, in reality, rebuilding, it will require planning permission. See, for example, *Young v First Secretary of State* (2004).

It may be claimed that the re-erection of a house would not be development if each part were pulled down and rebuilt in stages, as each stage would be a separate act of improvement within the exception in section 55(2). Although admitting it was theoretically possible, Lord Parker CJ stated in *Sainty v Minister of Housing and Local Government* (see 2.8.2.1) that it would rarely occur because it would be uneconomic to carry it out over a sufficiently long period to claim that each stage was a mere improvement and no more. A similar argument was tried and failed in *Larkin v Basildon District Council* and *Hewlett v Secretary of State for the Environment (No. 2)*.

Larkin v Basildon District Council (1980)

The appellant constructed two new external walls to a bungalow. He then sought to build the other two walls thereby obtaining a rebuilding of the house without having to comply with the height and size limits imposed on improvements to dwellinghouses under the *Town and Country Planning General Development Order* 1977 ('GDO 1977'). None of the original external walls remained. Part of the floor, the roof and some internal supporting walls remained. The Divisional Court upheld the Secretary of State's decision that the works amounted to the construction of a new dwelling rather than the improvement of the existing one.

Hewlett v Secretary of State for the Environment (No. 2) (1985)

The appellant owned a small building with only three walls. He jacked up the roof, undertook certain operations to the walls in turn, then worked on the roof itself. He claimed that as each stage of the work was merely an improvement, the fully improved building must be the same building, albeit improved. The Divisional Court noted that this claim was inconsistent with *Sainty* and *Larkin*. It is a matter of fact and degree, not a question of law, for the Secretary of State to determine whether the works amount to improvements or the construction of a new building.

1.4 ENGINEERING OPERATIONS

Engineering operations are not defined except as including 'the formation or laying out of means of access to highways' (section 336). So it is principally a matter of fact and degree whether works, other than such access works, amount to engineering operations.

Coleshill and District Investment Co v Minister of Housing and Local Government (1969)

The appellants acquired disused explosives stores buildings. The buildings were protected by blast walls and embankments. The appellants removed the embankments and proposed removing the blast walls. The Minister determined:

- that the removal of the embankments was an engineering operation; and

- that the removal of the blast walls was an alteration of the buildings and one which would materially alter the external appearance of the buildings.

The House of Lords held that the questions before the Minister were largely matters of fact and degree. Given the magnitude of the work of demolition of the embankments the Minister could reasonably regard that as constituting an engineering operation.

'Engineering' has its ordinary meaning and is not restricted to civil engineering.

Fayrewood Fish Farms Ltd v Secretary of State for the Environment and Hampshire County Council (1984)

F excavated and removed topsoil and other materials from agricultural land to construct fishponds. He claimed that the works were engineering operations for the purposes of agriculture (fish farming) and were therefore permitted development under the GDO 1977. (The current Order is different in this respect.) The planning inspector took the then Department of the Environment line that engineering operations would normally be the exercise of civil engineering skills in the construction of a specific project of sufficient size and shape that it can be illustrated by a plan or drawing with, where necessary, explanatory notes. On appeal to the High Court, the judge thought that this went too far. Although the existence of a plan could constitute important evidence, it was not essential. The judge also stated that the term 'engineering operations' should be given its ordinary meaning in the English language, so the engineering skills required were not necessarily those of a civil engineer. Nor was it necessary that an engineer be actually engaged on the project. Accordingly, the matter was remitted to the Secretary of State.

Although something may be fairly described as an engineering operation when looked at as a whole, it does not follow that no building results. So a reservoir embankment may be a building, even though the construction of the reservoir could be regarded as an engineering operation.

South Oxfordshire District Council v Secretary of State for the Environment and Keene (1986)

A farmer contended that the construction of a 500,000 gallon reservoir for irrigation was an engineering operation for the purposes of agriculture and so permitted by the GDO 1977. The local planning authority contended that it was a building operation, in which case it breached the size limits in the GDO (the embankment was too big). The Secretary of State upheld the farmer's claim and the local authority appealed.

The High Court stated that the Secretary of State seemed to have jumped to the conclusion that because something could more accurately be called an engineering operation than a building operation, then no building could have resulted. This was wrong. He should have considered whether the embankment was a building (a structure or erection) and so the case was remitted to him.

1.5 MINING OPERATIONS

Mining operations are defined in the *Town and Country Planning (General Permitted Development) Order* 1995 ('GPDO') as 'the winning and working of minerals in, on, or under land, whether by surface or underground working'. They also include the removal of material from certain deposits, such as slag heaps – section 55(4).

Mining operations are continuing operations, so commencement more than four years ago does not grant immunity to extractions since then.

Thomas David (Porthcawl) v Penybont Rural District Council (1972)

The appellants had the benefit of a licence to excavate a large area of coastal land in South Wales. The appellants commenced the extraction of sand and gravel from two areas within the licensed area without planning permission. More than four years after the extraction commenced, the local planning authority served an enforcement notice requiring the extraction to cease and the areas to be restored. The appellants claimed that as the mining operation had begun more than four years previously it was now immune from enforcement action and they could continue to extract more sand and gravel.

The Court of Appeal held that mining operations are continuing operations, and that each shovelful is a separate act of development. Therefore there is no right to continue the extraction, and any extraction within the last four years can be required to be restored.

1.6 OTHER OPERATIONS

It is uncertain what this means. However the operational limb of development means something that alters the physical characteristics of the land or what is under it or the air above it (*Cheshire County Council v Woodward*, see 1.2 above). Something meeting this definition which is not building, engineering or mining, could be an 'other operation'.

1.7 MATERIAL CHANGE OF USE

'Material' is not defined in the 1990 Act, but certain specified changes of use are deemed to be development and certain others are deemed not to be (below). In respect of any change of use outside these categories, it is a question of fact and degree whether that change is material. In determining this question, the decision maker must have regard to planning considerations, for the change must be 'material for planning purposes' (Lord Parker CJ, *East Barnet UDC v British Transport Commission*, see 1.7.1 below).

Questions of fact are matters for the relevant decision maker. The courts cannot overturn a finding of fact unless, on the evidence, no reasonable tribunal of fact could have made such a finding. Nevertheless the judicial approach to questions of materiality has thrown light on the meaning of the word. Furthermore, certain 'tools of analysis', in the words of the authors of the *Encyclopedia of Planning Law and Practice*, have been used by the courts.

1.7.1 Character of use of land not purpose of particular occupier

East Barnet Urban District Council v British Transport Commission (1962)

The British Transport Commission (BTC) acquired land that had been used by railway companies for stacking railway coal. Vauxhall Motors took leases of the land in order to use it as a transit depot for the handling and storage of cars in boxes. Ninety-nine per cent of the cars were moved by rail and they were usually stacked for between 4 and 14 days. The local planning authority served enforcement notices on BTC and Vauxhall requiring use as a transit depot to cease. The justices determined that use as a transit depot was not development and quashed the notices. The authority appealed to the Divisional Court.

In dismissing the appeal Lord Parker CJ said:

'... what one is really considering is the character of the use of the land and not the particular purpose of a particular occupier.

The mere fact that the commodity changes does not necessarily mean that the land is being used for a different purpose nor, as it seems to me, is there any relevance in the fact that the purpose for which the land is used is effected by other hands, in this case by [Vauxhall] and their employees.'

(Lord Parker accepted that use as a transit depot may be intensification (see 1.7.6), but noted that that is a matter of fact and degree for the justices.)

Westminster City Council v British Waterways Board (1984)

Westminster City Council had a lease of land that it used primarily as a street-cleansing depot. The use entailed a mixed and fluctuating use of land and buildings for workshops, offices, stores, staff facilities, and parking for street cleaning and other vehicles. The land was part of a large site owned by British Waterways who wished to terminate the Council's lease on the ground (under the *Landlord and Tenant Act* 1954) that they intended to occupy the premises for their own business of a marina. Planning permission would be required for this use. The Council objected that such permission would not be forthcoming as it would be desirable to preserve the existing street cleansing use.

The House of Lords held that the current use was not restricted to a street-cleansing depot as the identity of the occupier who carries on the use is irrelevant.

There was a mixture of uses that could be carried on by a wide variety of businesses operating some kind of vehicular transport. It was of no relevance to inquire what purpose the vehicles were used for when they left the site. Therefore the Council's real ground of objection was not the desirability of preserving a particular use, but the desirability of preserving their own occupation. This is not a legitimate planning ground.

Lewis v Secretary of State for the Environment (1971)

The appellant acquired a Dutch barn and adjacent workshop that had been used for the repair and maintenance of a fleet of vehicles in connection with a butcher's business. The appellant used the site for her motor repair business. Lord Widgery CJ stated that he could not detect any difference between the activity before and after the appellant had acquired the premises other than that the ownership of the vehicles was different. A mere change in identity could not constitute a material change of use and the Secretary of State had erred in law in holding to the contrary.

Lord Widgery's statement in *Lewis* should not be taken to mean that if the type of activity remains the same a material change of use could never occur. As he himself acknowledged in *Jones v Secretary of State for the Environment,* an ancillary use which becomes a primary use may constitute a material change, and an intensification of use can, in certain circumstances, be material (see 1.7.6).

Jones v Secretary of State for the Environment (1974)

A site had been used for a road haulage business. Trailers had been manufactured on site for use in connection with the business. The haulage business was sold and the site became used mainly for the large-scale manufacture of trailers for sale. The local planning authority served an enforcement notice requiring the manufacture of trailers to cease. The appellant claimed, following *Lewis*, that the activity was the same, and it could not make any difference from a planning point of view that in one instance the trailers were made for use by the maker, and in another they were being made for sale.

The Divisional Court disagreed and distinguished the *Lewis* case. This was not the case of a primary use surviving with a mere change in the personality of the user. Lord Widgery CJ observed that there was a change from a haulage use with ancillary trailer manufacture, to a new primary use of trailer manufacture.

1.7.2 The primary or predominant use must be determined

Shephard v Buckinghamshire County Council (1966)

From 1952 to 1964 residential premises had been leased to the United States Government for use by its air force. The premises had a high security use including use as a signals unit, but it had been put to administrative purposes also. In his decision, Mr Justice Goff stated that:

> '... one must look at the unit as a whole and see what is the predominant nature of the user.'

In applying this test, he found on the facts that the receiving and sending of secret messages was not the predominant use, and that the premises were an administrative unit for military purposes. The premises therefore fell within the meaning of 'office for any purpose' within Class II of the *Town and Country Planning (Use Classes) Order* 1963.

London Residuary Body v Secretary of State for the Environment (1989)

One of the key issues in this case was whether County Hall, the seat of the former Greater London Council ('GLC'), had use rights as offices within the *Use Classes Order* 1987 or whether the GLC's use was *sui generis* (unclassified) so that a change to office use could be material.

In the Court of Appeal Lord Justice Slade approved the planning inspector's statement that:

> 'where one has a complicated situation as is the case at County Hall, it is agreed that one needs to determine the primary purpose of the use.'

The inspector considered that, although most of the premises were used as offices, the primary use was governmental, with the distinct characteristics of an elected government use including: public debate and decision making, voting lobbies and party politics, press gallery, public meetings, public involvement and public access, etc. Accordingly Lord Justice Slade found the inspector entitled to regard the predominant use as not being as an office in the relevant sense.

Crawley Borough Council v Hickmet Ltd (1998)

The established use of the appeal site was commercial storage. The respondents began to use it for car parking for passengers flying out of Gatwick Airport. The local planning authority sought an injunction restraining the respondents from using the site for car parking. The respondents contended that the parking of cars whilst their owners were abroad amounted to commercial storage.

At first instance, the judge concluded that parking amounted to commercial storage. The Court of Appeal held that the judge had made an error of law. It was necessary, as a matter of planning law, to determine the use of the land. This required examining the activity, assessing the primary purpose to which the land was being put and deciding whether it could fairly be called 'storage'. The activity clearly indicated a primary use of land for car parking and not storage. Parking of cars for two to three weeks was not sufficient to constitute storage. It is an incident in the normal use of a car as it is being used for transport to and from the airport.

1.7.3 General and particular purposes

A change in general purpose (e.g. commercial to retail) will normally be material. Changes in the particular purpose within the same general purpose may fall within the *Use Classes Order* (e.g. butcher to baker) in which case there is deemed to be no development (below). If a change in a particular purpose is not within the Order, the question whether there is a material change of use is a matter of fact and degree in the circumstances of the case. It is, for example, an error of law to say that different types of residential use cannot be development because the general purpose is still residential.

Birmingham Corporation v Minister of Housing and Local Government and Habib Ullah (1964)

In this case there was a change from a single-dwellinghouse to a house in multiple occupation (a house-let-in-lodgings). The local planning authority served an enforcement notice alleging a material change of use and on appeal the Minister quashed the notice. The Minister's approach was that there can, as a matter of law, be no material change of use where a house is still used as a place where people dwell, albeit the purpose for which the house is used is different.

In the Divisional Court, Lord Parker CJ said that the minister had erred in law. He referred to his own decision in the *East Barnet* case (1.7.1 above) where he had asked the question:

> 'Does one consider the general purpose or does one have to descend to the particular and say: Was the particular purpose different?'

This question is one of fact and degree to be answered on the evidence in the case. He stated that:

> 'it would be very odd if one could not go further than merely determine that because it is residential that is an end of the matter.'

Whether the character of the use of a dwellinghouse as a private residence has been changed so substantially as to amount to a material change of use is a matter of fact and degree.

Blackpool Borough Council v Secretary of State for the Environment and Keenan (1980)

A solicitor bought a second home in Blackpool. It was empty for eight months of the year, but was used in the months of

15

July to October by the solicitor and his family, his friends, and also by 'family groups' who paid rent. The local planning authority served an enforcement notice alleging a material change of use to holiday lettings on a commercial basis. On appeal the inspector found that the house was occupied by family groups as single households, and so its use was not analogous to that of hotels or boarding houses, but was in accordance with the permitted use as a private dwellinghouse. The local authority challenged the decision, citing the *Habib Ullah* case, but the High Court found no error of law. The house was not constantly let on short holiday lettings, but was let to single households for ten weeks in the year. The inspector was entitled to find, as a matter of fact and degree, that the character of the house and its use was not materially changed by the succession of occupiers over the ten-week period.

A change from one type of residential use to another may be material because it gives rise to important planning considerations, such as a reduction in a type of accommodation, strain on welfare services, etc.

Panayi v Secretary of State for the Environment and Hackney London Borough Council (1985)

The case concerned the use of four self-contained flats to provide accommodation for the homeless. The planning inspector had found that there had been a material change of use of the flats to a hostel. Mr Justice Kennedy held that it was open to the inspector to come to this decision because the change could give rise to important planning considerations and could affect, for example, the residential character of the area, strain the welfare services, and reduce the stock of private accommodation available for renting. The fact that, in the broadest sense, the property continued to be used for residential purposes did not mean that there could not have been a material change of use.

1.7.4 Ancillary or incidental uses

The courts have developed the principle that the commencement of an ancillary or incidental use is not normally a material change of use as it is part and parcel of the primary use. (For cases on uses ancillary to agriculture and forestry, see 1.7.9.2.)

The courts interpret ancillary in the narrow sense of 'ordinarily incidental'.

Harrods Ltd v Secretary of State for the Environment, Transport and the Regions (2002)

Harrods claimed that the use of the store roof, for the taking off and landing of a helicopter for its chairman to get to and from work, was ancillary as there was a functional connection between the landing pad and the primary use. The local authority claimed that the use of the roof in this way was a material change of use and the Secretary of State agreed.

In upholding the Secretary of State's decision Lord Justice Schiemann said:

> 'The right approach is to see what shops in general have as reasonably incidental activities.'

His reasoning was that:

> '... if what an appellant wants to introduce is not generally associated with what goes on in shops then it seems probable that Parliament intended that neighbours should have the chance to object to the grant of planning permission and thus force the owner to go through the appropriate procedures to get his planning permission.'

Loss of ancillary status

If an ancillary use ceases to be so, it may amount to a material change of use.

Peake v Secretary of State for Wales (1971)

The appellant used a garage for the repair of his car and occasionally his friends' cars. On being made redundant he started repairing cars on a full-time basis. It was held that although mere change from part-time to full-time could not be material, there was a change in character of the use from dwellinghouse and ancillary garage to dwellinghouse and commercial garage. This entitled the Secretary of State to conclude that there had been a material change of use.

1.7.5 Dual and multiple uses

Ancillary uses must be distinguished from dual or multiple primary uses that are not subordinate to a single main use and are unrelated to each other. Multiple uses are usually called composite uses if they are not physically separate and distinct.

The mere abandonment or cessation of one of these uses cannot amount to a material change of use, but a material change may occur if one use expands to absorb the others.

Wipperman & Buckingham v London Borough of Barking (1965)

Between 1958 and 1961 a site was used for storage of farming materials, storage of building materials and a residential caravan for a person working on the land.

In 1961 the caravan use gave way to a car-breaking use. In 1962, the car-breaking use ceased, and the whole of the site was given over to the storage of building materials. An enforcement notice was served alleging a material change of use.

The court held that merely to cease one of the component activities in a composite use of the land would not, by itself, ever amount to a material change of use. But in this case the storage use had taken over the whole of the planning unit and this was capable of being a material change, provided the use absorbed was not so trifling as to be *de minimis*.

1.7.6 Intensification of use

Increase or intensification of use is capable, in appropriate circumstances, of constituting development.

Guildford Rural District Council v Penny (1959)

The appellants increased the number of caravans on a 1.5-acre caravan site from 8 to 27. The justices found that this did not constitute a material change of use. The Divisional

Court held that, as a question of fact, the justices were entitled to come to the conclusion they did. Lord Evershed MR observed, however, that intensification may affect a definable character of the land or of its use. He also regarded the consequent impact on local services as relevant:

'It is also, as it seems to me, obvious that increasing intensity of use or occupation may involve a substantial increase in the burden of services which a local authority has to supply, and that in truth might, in some cases at least, be material in considering whether the use of the land has been materially changed.'

Brooks and Burton v Secretary of State for the Environment (1978)

The Court of Appeal upheld the view of the Divisional Court in the *Guildford* case and confirmed that whether intensification is material is a question of fact:

'We have no doubt that intensification of use can be a material change of use. Whether it is or not depends on the degree of intensification. Matters of degree are for the Secretary of State to decide.'

In *Royal Borough of Kensington and Chelsea v Secretary of State for the Environment* Lord Justice Donaldson distinguished between the ordinary meaning of the word intensification – more of the same – and the meaning in planning language.

Kensington and Chelsea Royal Borough Council v Secretary of State for the Environment and Mia Carla Ltd (1981)

The appellant owned a restaurant on the ground floor of a building. He began to use the adjacent garden for the purposes of the restaurant. The planning authority served an enforcement notice alleging a material change of use from garden to restaurant. However, this notice was based on the false assumption that the garden was part of the residential accommodation above the restaurant. In fact it belonged to the same planning unit as the restaurant, so the notice should have alleged intensification. (Today the notice could be amended, see Chapter 4.) In commenting on the drafting of enforcement notices concerned with intensification, Lord

Justice Donaldson said that the word 'intensification' should be used with very considerable circumspection as intensification which did not amount to a material change of use was mere intensification and outside planning control.

1.7.6.1 Ancillary or incidental uses

The intensification of an ancillary use may amount to a material change of use if it creates a new primary use or a dual use.

Jones v Secretary of State for the Environment (1974)

Lord Widgery CJ observed that just as intensification of an activity can result in a material change of use, so if an ancillary use 'becomes level to the standard of a primary use', that may justify an allegation that a material change of use has occurred.

Hilliard v Secretary of State for the Environment (1979)

The owner of a farm obtained permission to erect a building subject to a condition that it should only be used for the storage of agricultural produce and farm implements in conjunction with the farm. The building became used for the wholesale distribution of fruit and vegetables. The local authority took enforcement action, not for breach of condition, but on the ground of intensification amounting to a material change of use.

The Secretary of State and the Divisional Court upheld the notice. (The Court of Appeal remitted the case to the Secretary of State, because the evidence had been directed to the intensification of the use of the building rather than the intensification of the use of the farm as a whole – the planning unit.)

1.7.7 The planning unit

In deciding whether a change of use is or is not a material change 'one must begin by deciding what is the planning unit' – Lord Widgery CJ in *Johnston v Secretary of State for the Environment* (1974).

The courts have employed the term 'planning unit' as:

'a useful piece of shorthand to describe the area of land or part of a building or group of buildings to which a local planning authority should properly have regard when considering whether there has been a material change of use in the use of any buildings or other land.' (Lord Justice Glidewell, *South Staffordshire District Council v Secretary of State for the Environment and Bickford* (1987))

The starting point, when considering what is the planning unit, is the unit of occupation.

Burdle v Secretary of State for the Environment (1972)

Mr Justice Bridge said:

'It may be a useful working rule to assume that the unit of occupation is the appropriate planning unit, unless and until some smaller unit can be recognised as the site of activities which amount in substance to a separate use both physically and functionally.'

The case concerned a scrap-yard on which stood a dwellinghouse. Attached to the house was a lean-to annexe. The lean-to had been used as an office in connection with the scrap business and incidental sales of car parts. The appellant started using the lean-to for the substantial retail sale of brand new vehicle parts. The planning authority served an enforcement notice alleging a material change of use.

The main issue before the Divisional Court was whether the planning unit was the lean-to or the whole of the site. The Secretary of State had held that, as a shop is a building, the word 'premises' in the enforcement notice must relate to the lean-to only. The Court disagreed. Mr Justice Bridge said:

'... what I cannot accept is that the accident of language which the planning authority choose to use in framing their enforcement notice can determine conclusively what is the appropriate planning unit ...'

He then sketched out three broad categories of distinction to help to determine the planning unit.

1   Where the occupier pursues a single main purpose to which secondary activities are incidental or ancillary, the whole unit of occupation should be considered to be the planning unit.

2   Where there are a variety of activities none of which are incidental or ancillary to another and which are not confined within separate and physically distinct areas of land, again the whole unit of occupation should normally be the planning unit. (This is usually said to be a composite use.)

3   Where within a single unit of occupation there are two or more physically separate and distinct areas occupied for substantially different and unrelated purposes, each area (together with its incidental and ancillary activities) should be a separate planning unit.

Wood v Secretary of State for the Environment (1973)

A conservatory attached to a farmhouse came to be used mainly for the sale of produce. It was alleged that the sale of imported produce had become so extensive as to amount to a material change of use. (The sale of homegrown produce was held to be ancillary.)

On appeal, the inspector considered that the increase in imported sales was not sufficient to be a material change in the use of the land. The Secretary of State, however, regarded the conservatory as a separate planning unit. He therefore came to the conclusion that there was a material change of use.

The Divisional Court held that this approach was an error of law. Referring to Mr Justice Bridge's starting point, Lord Widgery CJ said that it can rarely if ever be right to dissect a single dwellinghouse and to regard one room in isolation as being an appropriate planning unit.

Fuller v Secretary of State for the Environment (1988)

The applicant occupied farms in excess of 2,000 acres. The holding consisted of a number of disparate pieces of land, some of them separated from each other by several miles. The local planning authority took enforcement action in respect of the storage of grain for commercial purposes on certain of the farms. In coming to his decision as to whether there was a material change of use, the Secretary of State did not regard the entire holding as one planning unit. The Court of Appeal upheld this decision. The identification of the planning unit is a question of fact and degree, first for the local planning authority and then for the Secretary of State to decide.

The planning unit in a block of flats or other multi-let property will normally be the individual flat or unit.

Johnston v Secretary of State for the Environment (1974)

Premises consisting of 44 garages had originally been used for housing taxis. Over time, some garages became let to individual tenants, and in some cases a tenant took two or more garages. The planning authority was concerned that some of the garages were being used for vehicle repairs and served enforcement notices. The notices were directed to individual garages or groups of garages in separate occupations. The owners alleged that the proper planning unit was the entirety of the 44 garages.

Lord Widgery CJ, giving the judgment of the Divisional Court, observed that the unit of occupation, although not conclusive, was of great importance. He drew an analogy with a block of flats. Lord Widgery said:

'I would have thought that in almost every case of a block of flats, the flats being let to separate and different tenants, the planning unit would be the flat in question.'

Church Commissioners for England v Secretary of State for the Environment (1995)

The issue in this case was whether the MetroCentre, a substantial enclosed shopping centre, was the planning unit or whether the individual shops were separate planning units. The Secretary of State regarded each individual unit as occupied in its own right and, therefore, applying the criteria in the *Burdle* judgment, considered that each unit was, as a matter of fact and degree, the planning unit. This approach was upheld on appeal.

Planning unit and planning history – extinguishment of use rights

As well as the planning unit, another judicial concept, that of a 'new chapter' (occasionally 'break' or 'change') 'in the planning history' of the site, has sometimes been employed to help determine materiality. It has normally been used in cases where a new building has been erected (with or without permission) and there is an issue as to whether the existing use rights on the land built upon have been extinguished by the building. Where the building is substantial, it may be regarded, depending on the facts, as a new chapter in the planning history, thereby creating a new planning unit without the previous use rights. Where no permission has been granted, it has a nil use. Where planning permission has been granted, the use rights are those derived from the permission.

Petticoat Lane Rentals Ltd v Secretary of State for the Environment (1971)

A cleared bombsite had been used for market trading for many years. In 1963 planning permission was granted for the erection of a building on the site. The building was constructed on pillars so that the ground floor was unenclosed and was, according to the planning permission, to be used for car parking and, on Sundays, for market trading. After the building was erected, the local planning authority took enforcement action in respect of the use of the ground floor for market trading on weekdays. The appellant, who had a lease of the ground floor, claimed the benefit of existing use rights.

The High Court held that the erection of the building had extinguished the existing use rights. An entirely new planning unit with no planning history had been created. Thereafter any use is a change of use that can be restrained by planning control, unless authorised by the permission.

Jennings Motors Ltd v Secretary of State for the Environment and New Forest District Council (1982)

The appellants occupied a half-acre site for the repair and maintenance of vehicles and the sale and hire of cars. They demolished a workshop and erected a new building in its place without planning permission. The new building covered about six per cent of the site. The local planning authority took enforcement action, but did not require the removal of the building. Instead they required the use of the new building to be discontinued on the basis that its use was a material change of use. The notice was upheld on the basis that a new building creates a new planning unit.

The Court of Appeal held that the erection of a building is merely one of the factors to be taken into account in determining whether there is a new chapter in the planning history or, and it means the same thing, a new planning unit. The new building was relatively small and merely replaced existing buildings. The case was remitted to the Secretary of State to reconsider his decision in the light of the Court's guidance as to the correct legal approach.

By a majority the Court also observed that, although the term 'planning unit' is somewhat confusing as it combines concepts of both geography and history, it is to be preferred to 'change in the planning history'.

1.7.8 Abandonment of use rights

The mere cessation of a use is not a material change of use for 'no one can make a man continue with a branch of his business if he does not wish' – Lord Justice Widgery in *Hartley v MHLG*, below. However, as existing use rights can be abandoned by non-use the resumption of that use may amount to a material change. It is a question of fact and degree whether the cessation amounts to abandonment or is a mere temporary suspension. Where the land has no other use, then the abandonment results in a 'nil use'.

Hartley v Minister of Housing and Local Government (1969)

A petrol filling station and an adjoining plot of land had been used for car sales. In 1961 the car sales ceased. In 1965 the property was sold to the appellant who began using the petrol station and the adjoining land for the sale of cars. The local planning authority took enforcement action alleging a material change of use and requiring the land to be used as a petrol station only.

In his judgment in the Court of Appeal Lord Denning MR said:

'The question in all such cases is simply this: has the cessation of use ... been merely temporary, or did it amount to an abandonment? ... If it amounted to abandonment it cannot be resumed unless planning permission is obtained ... Abandonment depends on the circumstances. If the land has remained unused for a considerable time, in such circumstances that a reasonable man might conclude that the previous use had been abandoned, then the tribunal may hold it to have been abandoned.'

As there was ample evidence to support the Minister's finding of abandonment, the appeal was dismissed.

Criteria for determining abandonment

These were considered by the Court of Appeal in *Hughes* below.

Hughes v Secretary of State for the Environment, Transport and the Regions (2000)

The Court of Appeal accepted that the following criteria are relevant to the determination of whether the use of a building has been abandoned:

- the physical condition of the building;

- the length of time for which the building had not been used for the relevant use;

- whether it had been used for any other purposes (such as intervening uses);

- the owner's intentions.

A bungalow had been unoccupied since 1963 and had fallen into decay. In 1990 Mr Hughes bought the building with a view to constructing a replacement dwelling. It was claimed on behalf of Hughes that the previous owner had not formed the intention to abandon the use. On the contrary he had contemplated letting it and had also attempted to get planning permission for a residential use. Nevertheless, the Court of Appeal held that the inspector had been entitled to conclude that residential use had been abandoned.

Lord Justice Kennedy said:

'... the intentions of the site's successive owners, although relevant, were not and could not be decisive, because, at the end of the day, the test must be the view to be taken by a reasonable man with knowledge of all the relevant circumstance.'

1.7.9 Statutory exclusions from material change of use – section 55(2)

The following changes of use are not taken to involve development.

1.7.9.1 Use of dwellinghouse for incidental purpose – section 55(2)(d)

'The use of any buildings or other land within the curtilage of a dwellinghouse for any purpose incidental to the enjoyment of the dwellinghouse as such.'

The test of whether the purpose is incidental is objective.

Wallington v Secretary of State for Wales and Montgomeryshire District Council (1991)

W kept in excess of 40 dogs at her house as a hobby. The local planning authority served an enforcement notice alleging a material change of use and requiring the number of dogs to be reduced to six. W's appeal was dismissed by the inspector, who determined the matter on the basis of whether it was reasonable to regard the keeping of so many dogs as incidental, or whether it was so significant as to constitute a separate use.

The Court of Appeal upheld the inspector's approach. In particular, the Court placed emphasis on the words 'as such' in the legislation. These words mean that the use must be incidental to the dwellinghouse as a dwellinghouse.

'The mere fact that an occupier may genuinely regard the relevant activity as a hobby cannot possibly suffice to prove by itself that the purpose is incidental to the enjoyment of the dwellinghouse as a dwellinghouse.' (Lord Justice Slade)

Thus an objective approach has to be made to the given facts. Of relevance might be the situation of the dwelling, its size, the nature and scale of the activity and other matters. As usual it is a question of fact and degree.

Dwellinghouse

Whether something is a dwellinghouse is a question of fact. A distinctive characteristic of a dwellinghouse is the provision of facilities for day-to-day private domestic existence.

Gravesham Borough Council v Secretary of State for the Environment and O'Brien (Michael W) (1984)

Planning permission was granted for the erection of a small, single-storey holiday chalet. It measured 20 feet by 17 feet and comprised a bedroom with kitchen and a living room. There was no bathroom or toilet. Planning conditions prohibited use for human habitation between 1 November and 28 February, but allowed furniture and household effects to be stored there during those months.

The owner added an extension claiming that, as the building was a dwellinghouse, it was permitted development under the GDO 1977. In an enforcement appeal the Secretary of State determined that it was a dwellinghouse and that decision was upheld in the High Court. Mr Justice McCullough stated that the issue is one of fact. A distinctive characteristic of a dwellinghouse was its ability to afford to those who used it the facilities required for day-to-day private domestic existence. He noted that the use to which a building is put may be relevant but is not conclusive. For example, a wooden shed consisting of an office, w.c. and washbasin could hardly be turned into a dwellinghouse because someone put furniture in it and lived there. He observed that the fact that a second home is not lived in all year does not prevent it from being a dwellinghouse. If it was a dwellinghouse for eight months it did not cease to be a dwellinghouse in the other four.

The *Gravesham* decision and approach was approved by the Court of Appeal in *Moore v Secretary of State* (1998).

Moore v Secretary of State for the Environment, Transport and the Regions (1998)

The outbuildings of a large Edwardian country house were converted into ten self-contained units of residential accommodation for the purpose of holiday lettings in the New Forest. The planning inspector did not regard the units as single dwellinghouses because they were not occupied as permanent homes. The Court of Appeal held, following *Gravesham*, that there was no such requirement. Nor do dwellinghouses cease to be used as such because they are managed as a whole for the commercial purpose of holiday or other temporary lettings. Had the correct test been applied the inspector could only have properly concluded that the ten units were being used as single dwellinghouses.

Curtilage

The extent of the curtilage of a building is a question of fact and degree in the circumstances of the case. There is no requirement that the curtilage must be marked off in any way.

Sinclair-Lockhart's Trustees v Central Land Board (1950)

In this case, Lord Mackintosh examined the meaning of 'curtilage' with reference to a decision of the House of Lords in *Caledonian Railway v Turcan* (1898). He said:

'This rather illuminating decision seems to show that ground which is used for the comfortable enjoyment of a house or other building may be regarded in law as being within the curtilage of that house or building and thereby as an integral part of the same, although it has not been marked off or enclosed in any way. It is enough that it serves the purposes of the house or building in some necessary or reasonably useful way.'

Skerritts of Nottingham Ltd v Secretary of State for the Environment, Transport and the Regions (2000)

The case concerned a stable block some 200 metres from a hotel, a listed building. The issue was whether it was within the curtilage of the hotel (and therefore subject to listed building control). The hotel company cited the authority of *Dyer v Dorset County Council* (1989) in support of their contention that curtilage means a small area of land. The Court of Appeal, while confirming the actual decision in *Dyer*, stated that the Court had gone further than necessary in expressing the view that the curtilage of a building must always be small. Where houses are 20 to the acre, then obviously curtilage is small as no piece of land can be in the curtilage of more than one building. But the curtilage of a substantial building is likely to extend to what are or have been, in terms of ownership and function, ancillary buildings. Physical layout is relevant also.

Collins v Secretary of State for the Environment (1989)

The appellant occupied a cottage within 4.5 acres of gardens. There were well-cut lawns near the dwellinghouse and rough grass, largely neglected, over the rest of the grounds. The appellant erected a summerhouse, without planning permission, in the rough part of the gardens. The High Court upheld the inspector's finding that the building was not on land that could be described as part of the curtilage, as the land on which it stood did not serve the dwellinghouse.

1.7.9.2 Agriculture and forestry uses – section 55(2)(e)

Agriculture is defined thus:

> '"agriculture" includes horticulture, fruit growing, seed growing, dairy farming, the breeding and keeping of livestock (including any creature kept for the production of food, wool, skins or fur, or for the purpose of its use in the farming of land), the use of land as grazing land, meadow land, osier land, market gardens and nursery grounds, and the use of land for woodlands where that use is ancillary to the farming of land for other agricultural purposes, and "agricultural" shall be construed accordingly.'

The use of land for a particular purpose includes ancillary or incidental activities (above). Therefore the placing of a mobile caravan for activities ancillary to agricultural use is not development, even though it may be unsightly.

Wealden District Council v Secretary of State for the Environment (1988)

A farm in an area of outstanding natural beauty was used for raising beef cattle. There were some farm buildings, but no farmhouse, on the land. The farm buildings were not weatherproof, so the farmer stationed a caravan for the storage and mixing of calf feed and to provide shelter for himself and his wife. The planning authority served an enforcement notice alleging a material change of use without planning permission.

The Court of Appeal noted that it had long been established that a caravan with wheels was not a structure but the placing of it on land may be a material change of use. On the facts, the caravan was not used for residential purposes but was for agricultural purposes ancillary to the breeding and keeping of livestock. Therefore no development had taken place.

Sale of produce is ancillary to the growing of that produce.

Williams v Minister of Housing and Local Government (1967)

A building was used for the sale of produce from a nursery. Enforcement action was taken when the owner began to use the building for the sale of imported produce. The Minister's view that use for agriculture necessarily includes the selling of products grown on the land, but not the sale of imported produce, was upheld by the court.

(Followed in *Wood v Secretary of State* (1973).)

Difficulties have arisen where the produce is subjected to some form of treatment or processing before sale. Is such a process truly ancillary? The Court of Appeal gave guidance in *Millington v Secretary of State* below.

Millington v Secretary of State for the Environment, Transport and the Regions (1999)

The appellant farmer started making wine from his own grapes and selling it to the public. The local authority served an enforcement notice alleging that the sale of wine and visits by the public was a material change of use. The Secretary of State determined that the processing and bottling was an industrial process and so the sale of the wine produced by that process was not ancillary to agriculture. He granted planning permission for the making of wine but upheld the notice in respect of sales and visits by members of the public.

The Court of Appeal held that the Secretary had erred in law. Lord Justice Schiemann stated that the proper approach to the question was to consider whether what the farmer was doing could, having regard to ordinary and reasonable practice:

- be regarded as ordinarily incidental to the growing of grapes;

- be included in the general term agriculture;

- be regarded as ancillary to normal farming activities;

- be regarded as reasonably necessary to make the product marketable or disposable to profit; or

- be said to have come to the stage where the operations cannot reasonably be consequential on the agricultural operations of producing the crop.

The case was therefore remitted to the Secretary of State, but the Court was of the opinion that the making of wine or cider or apple juice on the scale in the case was perfectly normal for a farmer growing grapes or apples.

It was conceded by the Secretary of State that the grant of permission to make wine, whilst upholding the enforcement notice preventing it being sold, was irrational.

Use of land and buildings as a stud farm is not agricultural. However, where land is primarily used for grazing horses, it falls within the words 'use of land as grazing land' whether the horses are carthorses or racehorses.

Belmont Farm v Minister of Housing and Local Government (1962)

The appellant used land and buildings for the breeding and training of horses for show jumping. It was held that such use does not fall within 'breeding and keeping of livestock', because the words in brackets immediately after that phrase – '(including any creature kept for the production of food, wool, skins or fur, or for the purpose of its use in the farming of land)' – indicate that the horses must be for the purpose of farming if they are not kept for food or skins.

Sykes v Secretary of State for the Environment (1981)

Land was used for grazing non-agricultural horses. This was held to fall within the meaning of 'use of land as grazing land' because, unlike the words 'breeding and keeping of livestock', there was nothing in the definition limiting it to animals used for the purposes of farming. The Court noted that whether land is primarily used as grazing land is a question of fact. Just because horses happen to graze on a piece of land does not make it grazing land if they are fed primarily by other means. (See, for example, *Fox v First Secretary of State* (2003) where racehorses were grazed but were also supplied with food.)

Forestry includes operations necessary to render the timber marketable and disposable, even if those operations are not within the plantation.

Farleyer Estate v Secretary of State for Scotland (1992)

The appellants used a piece of land, 1,500 metres from their forestry plantation, as a timber storage and transfer area. Access to the site from the plantation was by a narrow and winding road through a small village.

The local planning authority served an enforcement notice alleging a change of use (storage and transfer) without planning permission. The reporter dismissed the appeal despite the fact that there was no alternative to the movement of timber along the road so that it could be stockpiled on the site and loaded on to lorries. His reasoning was that the site could not be ancillary as it was so physically divorced from the forest.

On appeal, the Court held that forestry includes operations necessary to render the timber marketable and disposable. This must include the extraction of the timber and its being stockpiled preparatory to its onward removal. It did not matter that the site was divorced from the plantation, as the use to which it was being put was that of forestry.

1.7.9.3 The Use Classes Order 1987 – section 55(2)(f)

'In the case of buildings or other land which are used for a purpose of any class specified in an order made by the Secretary of State under this section, the use of the buildings or other land or, subject to the provisions of the order, of any part of the buildings or the other land, for any other purpose of the same class.'

The purpose of the *Use Classes Order* 1987 is not to define development, but the opposite: it provides that a change of use within the same use class is not development. It makes no provision for changes that are not within the same class.

Rann v Secretary of State for the Environment and Thanet District Council (1980)

Mr and Mrs Rann owned a three-storey building that had planning permission as a hotel/guesthouse (Class XI of the *Use Classes Order* 1972). They began to use it for holiday accommodation for mentally handicapped people. The local planning authority claimed that this was a change of use to Class XIV and served an enforcement notice. Class XIV was: 'use as a home or institution providing for the boarding, care and maintenance of children, old people or persons under a disability, a convalescent home, a nursing home or a hospital'. The Secretary of State upheld the notice, so the Ranns appealed to the High Court on the ground that the use did not fall within Class XIV.

In his decision, Sir Douglas Frank QC observed that the *Use Classes Order* was being borrowed for a purpose for which it was not intended. Its purpose is not to define certain kinds of development, but to put outside the ambit of development a change of use within the same use class. He went on to conclude that the Ranns' use was not within Class XIV (because the word 'home' connotes permanence) but it did not necessarily follow that it was within Class XI. However, he did not have to decide this point.

Although the *Use Classes Order* applies to 'buildings or other land', certain words in some of the classes, such as 'hall' or 'hotel', indicate that a use must be within a building. See also *Cawley v Secretary of State for the Environment* (1990) as to the heading 'shops' in class A1, below.

The burden of proving that a use falls within the Order is upon the person relying upon it.

Rugby Football Union v Secretary of State for the Environment, Transport and the Regions (2001)

The Court of Appeal held that an open stadium, not being an enclosed space within a building, could not be a 'concert hall' within class D2(b).

The Court also observed that as section 55(2)(f) provides an exception to the general principle that any material change of use is development, it follows that if a landowner wishes to rely upon the *Use Classes Order*, the burden of proof must be upon him to show that his change of use comes within it.

When considering whether a change from a classified use to an unclassified use is material, the new use must be compared with the existing use, not the most intensive use that might be permissible within the relevant use class. Just because something is lawful if taken in two small steps, does not make it lawful in one large step. It is the materiality of the change that has to be considered.

Secretary of State for Transport, Local Government and the Regions v Waltham Forest London Borough Council (2002)

The proposed use of a large dwellinghouse was for six persons recovering from mental ill health living together as a single household with a minimum of one carer. Class C3 of the *Use Classes Order* 1987 includes use by a family and use by up to six persons living as a single household. The change would therefore not fall within the class, as there would be seven or eight occupiers including carers. In determining whether the proposed change was material, the inspector compared it with a large family or group of people that might live as a single household in such a dwellinghouse. (There was no evidence as to the number of persons currently occupying the house.)

The Court of Appeal held that the inspector had made an error of law. To interpose a notional permitted use between the existing use and the use applied for is not relevant. Lord Justice Schiemann drew an analogy with intensification. To move from intensity x to 2x may not be a material change of use. Nor to move from 2x to 3x. Nor from 3x to 4x and so on up to infinity. It does not follow that a change from x to 100x is not material.

Intensification of a classified use does not take it outside the use class.

Brooks and Burton v Secretary of State for the Environment (1978)

Land and buildings had been used between 1963 and 1973 for the making of concrete blocks without planning permission. No enforcement action had been taken, so the use was immune. The appellants took over the business, modernised it, and increased production significantly. Enforcement action was taken and, on appeal, the Secretary of State held that the new working procedures and the intensification of capacity was a material change of use.

The Court of Appeal held that as the whole site was a 'general industrial building' under Class IV of the old *Use Classes Order*, the intensification was still within this use class and so the owners were entitled to the benefit of what is now section 55(2)(f).

Ancillary or incidental uses

Article 3(3) of the *Use Classes Order* provides that a use which is 'included in and ordinarily incidental' to a use within a use class is not excluded from that use, even if it is specified in the Order as a separate use. Thus storage may be ancillary to retail although these uses are in separate classes.

Lord Justice Schiemann commented on the operation of this article in the *Harrods* case.

Harrods Ltd v Secretary of State for Environment, Transport and the Regions (2002)

The chairman of Harrods wished to use the store roof as a landing pad for a helicopter to travel to and from work. It was contended that the landing pad was reasonably incidental to the business of the shop.

In reaching his decision, Lord Justice Schiemann stated that the *Use Classes Order* was of no direct application to the case. Of article 3(3) he said:

'Its function is to prescribe that the fact that a use appears in a class of its own does not affect the operation of the ancillary use rule. However, it can be observed that it does proceed from the premise that one can in general do whatever is ordinarily incidental to the main use.'

Conditions restricting the operation of the Use Classes Order

Provided that there are planning reasons, a condition may be attached to the grant of permission prohibiting a change of use that would otherwise be permitted under the *Use Classes Order*.

City of London Corporation v Secretary of State for the Environment (1971)

The appellant had applied for planning permission for the change of use of a warehouse to an employment agency. The local planning authority granted permission on condition that the premises should be used as an employment agency only. This was to prevent the premises being turned into ordinary offices with a dead frontage and the loss of shop floor area in the City of London.

The appellant claimed that a condition could not be imposed to restrict a use which was not development.

The High Court upheld the condition. The statutory power to impose conditions regulating the use of land is not limited to activities that constitute development. So a condition may prohibit uses even though they would not amount to development.

Sui generis uses

In this context *sui generis* means a use that is unclassified. So a change to or from a *sui generis* use is outside the Order. The *Use Classes Order* itself sets out a list of *sui generis* uses in article 3(6), but it is not exhaustive and the courts have identified various *sui generis* uses, as in the *Tessier* case.

Tessier v Secretary of State for the Environment (1976)

A barn had been used for some years as a sculptor's studio. It was equipped for this purpose with benches, an anvil and other equipment, and lead, brass and other material had been worked on. The barn was acquired by the appellant who used it for vehicle maintenance and servicing. He claimed that the use as a studio was a general industrial building under Class IV of the *Use Classes Order* 1972 and that the current use was within the same class.

In the Divisional Court Lord Widgery upheld the Secretary of State's finding that the studio use was *sui generis*. He also stated that the use classes should not be stretched to embrace activities which clearly did not fall within them.

Mixed uses

The *Use Classes Order* has no application to a mixed use.

Belmont Riding Centre v First Secretary of State and London Borough of Barnet (2003)

The appellant claimed that the planning unit had existing use rights as a riding centre. He therefore claimed that a change to a health and fitness centre would not be development if both uses were in class D2.

It was determined that use as a riding centre existed, if at all, as one of a number of mixed uses across the whole planning unit, including agricultural and residential uses. Mr Justice Richards rejected the argument that there is no material change if one component of the mixed use falls within D2 and is replaced by another use within D2. The focus is on the mixed use as a whole, not the individual components of a mixed use.

'The use classes order has no application to a mixed use: the mixed use does not itself fall within any class and a finding of material change of use is not avoided simply by showing that a component falling within a particular class has been substituted for another component falling within the same class.'

(Approved by the Court of Appeal in *Fidler v First Secretary of State* (2004).)

Class A1 – shops

This includes retail sale of goods (other than hot food), the display of goods for sale, and certain other specified activities. The class is limited to the sale, display or service to visiting members of the public.

Certain retail uses, such as petrol stations, sale of motor vehicles, retail warehouse clubs and nightclubs, are excluded by article 3(6).

The meaning of 'shops' has been examined by the courts.

Cawley v Secretary of State for the Environment and Vale Royal District Council (1990)

The appellant owned open land which had planning permission for use as a garden centre. He began to use the land for the sale of caravans, claiming that both uses were within class A1.

The judge noted that subordinate legislation is laid before Parliament by the relevant minister. So the heading 'shops' was part of the language used by the maker of the Order. Therefore class A1 only applies to buildings. To hold that it applied to open land would make a nonsense of the word 'shops'.

The changing of currency and travellers' cheques is not the retail sale of goods.

Palisade Investments Ltd v Secretary of State for the Environment (1995)

The appellant claimed that a bureau de change was within class A1 as the buying and selling of currency was a retail use. The Court of Appeal disagreed. There was no 'retail sale of goods', but rather an exchange of money. Furthermore, a bureau de change comes within A2, the provision of financial services.

As noted above, mixed uses fall outside the use class. The fact that the primary use remains retail does not mean that different uses can be introduced alongside. Retail sale means retail and ancillary activities only.

Lydcare Ltd v Secretary of State for the Environment (1984)

The appellant began to use the basement of a shop for the viewing of films in eight coin-operated cubicles. Such a use was not ancillary, so it was contended instead that, so long as the primary use was still retail, the use was still as a shop. Thus the film use, even though a material change, would not take the premises outside the use class. This contention was based on the wording of the *Use Classes Order* 1972, which included the phrase: 'wherein the primary purpose is selling of goods by retail'.

The contention was not accepted by the Court of Appeal. The words 'primary purpose' were restrictive, not enlarging.

(The wording of the current order renders this argument clearly unsustainable.)

Class A2 – financial and professional services

'Use for the provision of:

(a)   financial services; or

(b)   professional services (other than health or medical services); or

(c)   any other services (including use as a betting office) which it is appropriate to provide in a shopping area,

where the services are provided principally to visiting members of the public.'

(Article 3(6) excludes taxi business and vehicle hire.)

It is a question of fact whether any particular service is provided principally to visiting members of the public.

The requirement that the use be 'appropriate to provide in a shopping area' only applies to 'other services' under paragraph (c).

Kalra v Secretary of State for the Environment and Waltham Forest Borough Council (1996)

A solicitor wished to open an office in a shopping area in Leyton in which, in general, only class A1 uses and appropriate A2 and A3 uses were permitted. He was refused permission on the ground that his use was a business use under class B1. He claimed he would be within class A2 on the basis that he would be providing a friendly, cheap and convenient access to legal advice to the North Indian ethnic community, whose language he spoke. He would not be doing conveyancing or commercial work.

The inspector had rejected his appeal, partly on the ground that a solicitor's office would not be 'appropriate to provide in a shopping area'. The Court of Appeal held that this was an error of law. The requirement that a service be appropriate in a shopping area only applies to paragraph (c) (other services) not financial or professional services. The issue was whether the solicitor would be providing services principally to visiting members of the public, rather as a law centre or Citizens' Advice Bureau does. This is an issue of fact. The use of a system of appointments does not necessarily mean that services are not provided principally to visiting members of the public. Hairdressers use appointments. If a solicitor could plausibly say that he intended to run an A2 office, and the local planning authority have no reason to disbelieve him, all they can do is grant permission and then monitor the situation.

The old A3 food and drink class has now been replaced by three new classes: A3, A4 and A5, so that the movement from restaurant to pub or takeaway is now constrained. See the associated changes to Part 3 of the GPDO, which permits movement between certain classes.

Class A3 – Restaurants and cafes

'Use for the sale of food or drink for consumption on the premises.'

Class A4 – Drinking establishments

'Use as a public house, wine bar or other drinking establishment.'

Class A5 – Hot food takeaways

'Use for the sale of hot food for consumption off the premises.'

Class B1 – Business

'Use for all or any of the following purposes:

(a) as an office other than a use within class A2;

(b) for research and development of products or processes; or

(c) for any industrial process.'

A class B1 use must be something that can be carried out in any residential area without detriment to amenity by reason of noise, vibration, smell, fumes, smoke, soot, ash, dust or grit.

Office use is not confined to commercial offices.

London Residuary Body v Secretary of State for the Environment (1989)

The Court of Appeal held that the Secretary of State was wrong to categorise class B1 of the *Use Classes Order* 1987 as limited to commercial offices. The word 'business' in the title does not have that effect. So offices for administering a charity, or military offices (as in *Shephard v Buckinghamshire County Council* (1966) at 1.7.2 above) may fall within class B1. However, on the facts, the government use of County Hall was *sui generis*.

An industrial use may fall within class B1 because of measures mitigating or eliminating emissions, notwithstanding that such a use would normally be considered to be a general industrial use.

Blight & White Ltd v Secretary of State for the Environment (1993)

A building had permission for the fabrication of structural steelwork and general engineering. The permission was subject to a condition that the premises should be used only for the purposes within Use Class III under the *Use Classes Order* 1972. (This was the old light industrial use with the same notional residential amenity test as now appears in class B1.) After the appellants took over the building, local residents on a nearby estate began to complain about noise. The local planning authority served enforcement notices alleging both breach of the condition and a material change of use. The appellants claimed that the condition was inconsistent with the permission which permitted a general industrial use and should be severed from it.

The High Court held that it was not self-evident that the permitted industrial activity must cause detriment to amenity by emissions, given the mitigating measures which might be put in place. The condition was a perfectly valid means of ensuring that noise and other emissions were at an acceptable level.

Class B2 – General industrial

'Use for the carrying on of an industrial process other than one falling within class B1 above ...'

(Classes B3 – B7 abolished.)

Class B8 – Storage or distribution

'Use for storage or as a distribution centre.'

There is no need for a business element.

Newbury District Council v Secretary of State for the Environment (1980)

Two aircraft hangars had been used to store civil defence vehicles during the 1950s. The House of Lords held that this use came within Class X of the *Use Classes Order* 1950, which included 'use as a wholesale warehouse or repository for any purpose'. So long as storage was the principal use, there need be no business element.

(The wording of class B8 indicates no change from this position.)

'Warehouse' under the old Class X was held not to imply retail use except in a limited incidental sense. Class B8 avoids the word warehouse altogether, leaving no doubt that retail use falls outside it.

Decorative and Caravan Paints v Minister of Housing and Local Government (1970)

A warehouse was used for substantial retail sales. The appellants claimed that 'warehouses shaded off into shops'. The Divisional Court upheld the Secretary of State's view that the building was not being used as a warehouse (under the old Class X) but as a shop.

Class C1 – Hotels

'Use as a hotel or as a boarding or guesthouse where, in each case, no significant element of care is provided.'

Hostels are *sui generis* under article 3(6)(i). Whether a building is being used as a hostel is a question of fact and degree.

Panayi v Secretary of State for the Environment and Hackney London Borough Council (1985)

Four self-contained flats were used for the accommodation of homeless families. The local planning authority served an enforcement notice alleging a material change of use to a hostel. The appellant claimed that the use was not that of a hostel as there was a lack of communal facilities as a whole, there were separate cooking and washing facilities and only a limited amount of cleaning services provided. After considering some definitions in statutes and case law (the latter emphasising modest accommodation, temporary in nature) Mr Justice Kennedy stated that he did not consider it necessary or even desirable to add to those definitions of the word hostel, which was an ordinary English word in common use. He saw nothing wrong with the Inspector's conclusion that at the material time the premises were being used as a hostel. Consequently, the Inspector was entitled to find, as a matter of fact and degree, that this change was material.

Class C2 – Residential institutions

'Use for the provision of residential accommodation and care to people in need of care (other than a use within class C3 (dwelling houses)).

Use as a hospital or nursing home.

Use as a residential school, college or training centre.'

Care is defined in article 2 as 'personal care for people in need of such care by reason of old age, disablement, past or present dependence on alcohol or drugs or past or present mental disorder, and in class C2 also includes the personal care of children and medical care and treatment'. (For a case on C2, see *North Devon District Council v First Secretary of State* (2003), considered under class C3, below.)

Class C3 – Dwellinghouses

'Use as a dwellinghouse (whether or not as a sole or main residence):

(a) by a single person or by people living together as a family; or

(b) by not more than six residents living together as a single household (including a household where care is provided for residents).'

The definition of care in article 2 is set out above under C2.

Care homes will normally fall within class C2, but where a community care home is small and the members constitute a single household it will fall within class C3(b).

Carers must be resident to form part of a single household, according to Mr Justice Collins in *North Devon District Council v First Secretary of State* (2003). He declined to follow Mr Justice Popplewell's approach to the contrary in *R v Bromley LBC, ex parte Sinclair* (1991).

North Devon District Council v First Secretary of State (2003)

A company leased a house to be used for the residential care of two children. The children were cared for on a rota basis by non-residential staff. The company sought a lawful use certificate on the basis that the new use fell within class C3(b). Mr Justice Collins held that the children could not form a household, as they were not capable of looking after themselves. He disagreed with the view in *R v Bromley* that a single household can include the non-residential staff. He stated that living together as a household requires that a proper functioning household exists, and so the children and carers must reside in the premises. Therefore the house was within class C2. It was a question of fact and degree whether the change from C3 to C2 was material.

Whether there is a single household or a house in multiple occupation is a matter of fact and degree. Much of the case law is under the *Housing Act* 1985, but the same judicial approach was taken to class C3 in *R (Hossack) v Kettering BC* (below).

Barnes v Sheffield City Council (1995)

A house was occupied by five students. The principal issue for the Court was whether it was in multiple occupation under the *Housing Act* 1985. Sir Thomas Bingham MR identified nine factors, in no particular order:

- the origin of the tenancy – whether the residents arrived as a single group or were independently recruited by the landlord;

- the extent to which the facilities were shared;

- whether the occupants were responsible for the whole house or just their particular rooms;

- the extent to which residents can and do lock their doors;

- the responsibility for filling vacancies – whether that of the existing occupants;

- the allocation of rooms – whether by the occupants or the landlord;

- the size of the establishment;

- the stability of the group;

- the mode of living – to what extent communal and to what extent independent.

Sir Thomas Bingham also referred to the judgment of Lord Hailsham in *Erin v Pizzey* (1979) to the effect that there is no single factor the presence or absence of which is by itself conclusive.

The absence of a pre-formed group may indicate multiple occupation, but is not conclusive. All factors have to be taken into account.

R (on the application of Hossack) v Kettering Borough Council and English Churches Housing Group (2002)

English Churches Housing Group maintained three adjoining terraced houses to provide temporary accommodation and support for small groups of up to six people in need – homeless, mentally ill, drug and alcohol addicts and the like. There were no separate cooking and eating facilities. Bathrooms were shared. The local planning authority determined that the use was within class C3. The matter came before the courts and turned on the question of whether each house was a single household.

The Court of Appeal held that although the absence of a pre-formed group may be indicative of multiple occupation it is not conclusive. Lord Justice Simon Brown observed that the smaller the number of occupants, the more intimate, integrated and cohesive their occupancy is likely to be. The matter was referred back to the council who, following the Court of Appeal's guidance, arrived at the same decision after further examination of the circumstances of the case.

Where there are more than six residents living as a single household, it is a matter of fact and degree whether this is a material change of use. In reaching a determination, the new use must be compared with the previous use, not the most intensive use that is permissible within the use class. Materiality is always judged in relation to the previous use.

Secretary of State for Transport, Local Government and the Regions v Waltham Forest London Borough Council (2002)

This case has been more fully considered above. In determining materiality, the proposed change of use as a dwellinghouse for seven or eight persons (including carers) had to be compared with the actual previous use, not a hypothetical large family or group of people living as a single household.

47

A change from a residential use outside class C3 to a single dwellinghouse is not a change within the use class. Therefore it may be development requiring planning permission.

Richmond upon Thames London Borough Council v Secretary of State for the Environment, Transport and the Regions (2000)

A house was converted into seven self-contained flats with the benefit of planning permission in 1970. In 1998 the owner applied for a certificate that the conversion back to a single dwellinghouse would be lawful. The certificate was refused.

The High Court held that as the flats were outside class C3, the conversion of the flats to a single dwellinghouse was not a change within the class. It could therefore be a material change of use if it gave rise to a planning consideration. The loss of residential property available for renting is such a consideration. The inspector had been wrong to concentrate on the impact on the building alone.

Class D1 – Non-residential institutions

'Any use not including a residential use:

(a)   for the provision of any medical or health services except the use of premises attached to the residence of the consultant or practitioner;

(b)   as a crèche, day nursery or day centre;

(c)   for the provision of education;

(d)   for the display of art (otherwise than for sale or hire);

(e)   as a museum;

(f)   as a public library or public reading room;

(g)   as a public hall or exhibition hall;

(h)   for, or in connection with, public worship or religious instruction.'

Class D2 – Assembly and leisure

'Use as:

(a)   a cinema;

(b)   a concert hall;

(c)   a bingo hall or casino;

(d)   a dance hall;

(e)   a swimming bath, skating rink, gymnasium or area for other indoor or outdoor sports or recreations not involving motorised vehicles or firearms.'

'Recreations' has been given a restricted meaning indicating some physical effort, not mere pleasurable enjoyment. The word 'hall' cannot include an open stadium.

Rugby Football Union v Secretary of State for the Environment, Transport and the Regions (2001)

The RFU claimed that their proposed use of Twickenham as a concert venue was within class D2. This raised two related issues. Assuming a rugby football stadium is within class D2(e) as use for outdoor sport or recreation, was its use as a concert venue within class D2(b)? If not, was use as a concert venue a recreation within class D2(e)?

The Court of Appeal held that an open stadium, not being an enclosed space within a building, could not be a 'concert hall'. Furthermore, a concert performance is neither sport nor recreation. To hold that recreation included any pleasant occupation, pastime or amusement (as in the OED definition) would render the rest of D2 otiose. Therefore the RFU's proposed use fell outside class D2.

1.7.9.4   Permitted changes from one use class to another – General Permitted Development Order

The *General Permitted Development Order* 1995 ('GPDO') grants permission for certain types of development. (See 2.8 for a fuller exposition.) Part 3 of Schedule 2 permits certain changes from one use class to another. They are changes to uses with less, or no greater, impact on amenity than the current use. For example, Part 3, class A permits change to class A1 from a use within class A3, class A4 or class A5.

Class D permits change to A1 from an A2 use with a ground floor display window. Whether a ground floor window can sensibly be described as a display window is a question of fact and degree.

North Cornwall District Council v Secretary of State for Transport, Local Government and the Regions (2002)

A double-fronted house with a matching pair of large, prominent bay windows was changed from office to retail. A planning inspector determined that the change was permitted development within class D of the GPDO and the planning authority appealed.

The inspector's approach was upheld in the High Court. There was no requirement that a display be designed as such and the inspector had considered such matters as sill heights, window area and glazing bars. It was impossible to say that his conclusion that they were display windows was unreasonable.

Part 3 of the GPDO and the 'ratchet'

The changes permitted by Part 3, classes A, B, C and D allow movement one way only, like a ratchet, whereas classes F and G specifically provide for movement both ways. This means, for example, that a change from B2 to B1 results in the loss of B2 use rights. Furthermore, if the owner changes back to B2 without planning permission, he will not be able to change back again to B1 because the GPDO does not apply to changes from unlawful uses.

Young v Secretary of State for the Environment (1983)

A large building was used as a laundry. This use fell within Class IV of the *Use Classes Order* 1972 (general industrial building). In 1969 the use changed to food processing within Class III (light industrial use). Such a change was permitted development. In 1970 the use reverted to that of a laundry and in 1977 the building was put back to light industrial use (the business of an insulating contractor).

The House of Lords determined that the reversion back to laundry use was development requiring planning permission. This meant that the building had no lawful use without obtaining planning permission (except for impractical uses such as agriculture) for to change back to light industrial use again would not be permitted by the GDO 1977. This was because it would be a change from an unlawful laundry use. So the current light industrial use was unlawful even though it was within Class III and the original use had been within Class IV.

(This decision has now been given statutory force in article 3(5)(b) of the GPDO, which provides that the Order is of no effect if the existing use is unlawful. Article 3(5)(a) is a similar provision about development in connection with an unlawful building operation.)

Does the ratchet always work?

Doubts have been cast upon the ratchet effect by the decision of the Court of Appeal in *Cynon Valley BC v Secretary of State for Wales* (1986). However, this decision has been questioned by the authors of the *Encyclopedia of Planning Law and Practice*, and may have been superseded because of the wording of article 3(2) in the GPDO.

1.7.10 Statutory inclusions

Section 55(3) sets out two changes of use which, 'for the avoidance of doubt', are deemed to be material.

1.7.10.1 Single dwelling to two or more separate dwellings – section 55(3)(a)

'The use as two or more separate dwellinghouses of any building previously used as a single dwellinghouse involves a material change in the use of the building and of each part of it which is so used.'

(Building includes any part of a building – section 336(1).)

A house may be occupied by persons living separately without consisting of separate dwellings.

Ealing Corporation v Ryan (1965)

A three-storey house was used to provide accommodation for three families of adults and children. In essence, the families occupied different floors, but shared a kitchen and, apparently, bathroom and toilet facilities. The local planning authority alleged a change from a single dwellinghouse to two or more separate dwellings. The magistrates decided that the dwellings were not separate and the High Court upheld their decision.

Mr Justice Ashworth stated that persons may live separately under one roof without occupying separate dwellings. Multiple occupation is not enough in itself. Relevant factors include the presence or absence of physical reconstruction and whether the dwellings are self-contained and independent, but this is by no means an exhaustive list and in every case it is a matter of fact and degree.

It does not follow that, because the change is only to multiple occupation and not to separate dwellings that the change is not material. It is a matter of fact and degree. See *Birmingham Corporation v Minister of Housing and Local Government and Habib Ullah* (1964), 1.7.3.

1.7.10.2   Waste on land – section 55(3)(b)

'The deposit of refuse or waste materials on land involves a material change of use, notwithstanding that the land is comprised in a site already used for that purpose, if:

(i)   the superficial area of the deposit is extended; or

(ii)   the height of the deposit is raised and exceeds the level of the adjoining land.'

The use of a quarry for back-filling waste during the quarrying process is entirely different from its use as a general tip. The latter is a material change of use.

Alexandra Transport Co v Secretary of State for Scotland (1972)

A planning permission for a quarry was subject to a condition that all overburden and waste materials should be back-filled into the quarry. When quarrying ceased, the owners sold the quarry as a tip. It was contended for the owners that as the tip was not being extended in height above ground level or in area it was not a material change of use. The Court of Session determined that the use as a tip for outside refuse was not the same use as back-filling, which was incidental to a mining operation. It was a material change of use from a quarry to a dump.

Note also that regulation 31 of the *Town and Country Planning (Environmental Impact Assessment) (England and Wales) Regulations* 1999 deems a change of use of land or a building for the purposes of incineration, chemical treatment or landfill of hazardous waste to be a material change of use.

1.7.10.3 Display of adverts – section 55(5)

The use for the display of advertisements of any external part of a building is a material change of use. (The advertisement regulations, under which advert consent constitutes deemed planning permission, are outside the scope of this book. See the *Town and Country Planning (Control of Advertisements) Regulations* 1992.)

1.7.10.4 Temporary sleeping accommodation in Greater London

In Greater London, the use of residential accommodation for the provision of sleeping accommodation for less than 90 consecutive nights is deemed to be a material change of use by section 25 of the *Greater London (General Powers) Act* 1973 (subject to certain provisions).

Fairstate Ltd v First Secretary of State (2005)

After ten years of uninterrupted use for temporary sleeping provision, a flat was occupied for 155 days by K under consecutive tenancies. Being more than 90 days, this amounted to residential occupation of a longer-term nature. On the resumption of temporary sleeping provision, the local planning authority served an enforcement notice. The owner claimed that the use for temporary sleeping provision, being lawful by virtue of ten years' use, could only be lost by abandonment or material change of use.

The Court of Appeal held that the wording of section 25 deemed there to be a material change of use when use for residential accommodation changed to temporary sleeping provision. So the issue of whether the intervening tenancy had amounted to a material change of use was irrelevant.

1.8 CERTIFICATES OF LAWFUL USE OR DEVELOPMENT – SECTIONS 191 AND 192

If a person wishes to establish that a particular use or development is lawful, he may apply to the local planning authority for a certificate to that effect. The applicant may appeal to the Secretary of State against a refusal and must prove his case on the balance of probabilities.

1.8.1 Informal determinations under the old provisions

It used to be the case that an application for planning permission for a proposed use or development was regarded as an informal application for a determination as to whether or not permission was required. The authority for this was *Wells v Minister of Housing and Local Government* (1967). The provisions under which *Wells* was decided have been replaced by a new and comprehensive code in sections 191 and 192. So the rule in *Wells* no longer applies (see the *Saxby* case, below). Furthermore, the House of Lords in the *Reprotech* case, below, has now cast doubt on the correctness of the *Wells* decision even under the law as it then was.

Saxby v Secretary of State for the Environment, Transport and the Regions and Westminster City Council (1998)

The applicant applied for planning permission for two dovecotes. Planning permission was refused by the local planning authority and by an inspector on appeal. The applicant challenged the decision, partly on the ground that no planning permission was required and that, on the authority of *Wells*, the planning authority had failed to determine whether planning permission was required.

The judge held that *Wells* no longer applied. The new law provides for a detailed scheme as to the matters to be comprised in an application for a determination. If the authority were able to determine whether planning permission is required as part of a planning application, it would sidestep the comprehensive scheme whose provisions are for the protection of the public as well as the applicant and the local authority.

1.8.1.1 Informal officer decisions

The case of *Lever (Finance) Ltd v Westminster Corporation* (1970) established that, in appropriate circumstances, a planning authority may be 'estopped' from denying a false statement made by a planning officer, with apparent but no actual authority, that planning permission was not required. (Estoppel prevents a person from going back on a statement or promise which another person has relied upon to his detriment.) However, it has now been established that estoppel, a creature of private law, is inappropriate to the public law of planning control, where statutory powers are exercisable in the interest of the public as a whole. The public law concept of 'legitimate expectation' is to be preferred.

R v East Sussex County Council, ex parte Reprotech (Pebsham) Ltd (2002)

Reprotech claimed that an officer's report to committee, or the committee's decision, constituted a determination, on the authority of *Wells*, that no planning permission was required to use a waste treatment plant to generate electricity.

The House of Lords held that the *Wells* case could be distinguished. (The committee in *Reprotech* did not actually decide whether or not permission was required.) More importantly, however, the House doubted the correctness of the *Wells* decision. And on the question of estoppel, not only did the House find no facts to justify an estoppel, but Lord Hoffman, delivering the unanimous judgment of the House, stated that 'it is unhelpful to introduce private law concepts of estoppel into planning law'. He preferred the public law concept of 'legitimate expectation' under which the denial of a legitimate expectation may amount to an abuse of power. This has advantages over estoppel in that the court can take account of the hierarchy of individual rights which exist under the *Human Rights Act* 1998. So, for example, the right to a home is accorded more protection than ordinary property rights. No legitimate expectation arose in this case.

Henry Boot Homes Ltd v Bassetlaw District Council (2002)

The Court of Appeal was not prepared to state that legitimate expectation could never operate so as to enable a developer to begin development in breach of condition. In circumstances where there is no third party or public interest in the matter it is possible that a legitimate expectation might arise. But 'such cases will be very rare'. (This case is examined in more detail in 2.2.1.)

1.8.2 Certificate of lawfulness of existing use or development – section 191

A certificate under section 191 may be sought for an existing use, for operational development that has taken place, or for any past breach of a condition or limitation. For example, a use, operation or activity may be lawful because the time limit for enforcement has expired.

The use, operation or non-compliance with a condition must exist at the time of the application for the certificate (see *Nicholson v Secretary of State for the Environment* (1998), below at 4.2.5).

Lawful

This means lawful under planning law.

East Dunbartonshire Council v Secretary of State for Scotland (1999)

It was claimed that the commencement of development (sight lines at a road junction) was not lawful as it required the consent of the owner, which was not available at the time. The Court held that the word 'lawful' looks primarily to the position under the planning legislation.

1.8.2.1 Scope of lawful uses

Westminster City Council v British Waterways Board (1984)

In the context of determining the scope of an established use, Lord Bridge said that it is necessary to answer two questions of fact:

'First, what is the precise character of the established use? Second, what is the range of uses sufficiently similar in character to the established use to be capable of replacing the established use without involving a material change?'

1.8.2.2 Time limits and the grant of Lawful Development Certificates

This topic is examined in the context of enforcement in Chapter 4 as it is bound up with the time limits in section 171B for taking enforcement action.

1.8.3 Certificates of lawfulness of proposed use or development – section 192

This allows a person to apply to the local planning authority for a determination as to whether a proposed use or development is lawful.

If so, the authority shall issue a certificate to that effect.

This procedure cannot be sidestepped. See the cases *Saxby v Secretary of State for the Environment, R v East Sussex CC, ex parte Reprotech* and *Henry Boot Homes Ltd v Bassetlaw DC* (at 1.8.1).

Section 192 does not empower a planning authority to make the issue of a certificate conditional upon a modification being made to the proposal.

R (on the application of Tapp) v Thanet District Council (2001)

Certificates were obtained in respect of the proposed use of a RAF airfield for civilian use. Local residents challenged the certificates on the basis that the planning authority had failed to consider the question of whether intensification could amount to a material change and so should have sought a limitation on the description of the development in the certificates.

The Court of Appeal held that it was not open to a local authority to require the modification of a section 192 application. However, in appropriate cases it could tell the applicant that the application was too wide and a more limited one might meet with more success.

2
Planning permission

2.1 THE REQUIREMENT OF PLANNING PERMISSION

Planning permission is required for the carrying out of development of land – section 57 of the *Town and Country Planning Act* 1990 ('the 1990 Act').

Planning permission may be granted unconditionally or subject to such conditions as the local authority think fit (section 70(1)). (The subject of planning conditions is dealt with in Chapter 3 as their imposition is often related to questions of materiality and validity.)

2.1.1 The effect of planning permission

Section 75 provides that planning permission enures for the benefit of the land and of all persons for the time being interested in it. It follows from this that, unlike existing use rights, planning permission cannot be abandoned, although it may become physically impossible to implement.

Pioneer Aggregates (UK) Ltd v Secretary of State for the Environment and Peak Park Joint Planning Board (1985)

In 1950 planning permission was granted for the mining and working of limestone. Quarrying ceased by 1967. In 1978 Pioneer Aggregates became interested in the site and asked the Board if planning permission was needed for quarrying. The Board replied to the effect that the planning permission had been abandoned. Pioneer challenged this decision.

The House of Lords held that, as planning permission enures for the benefit of the land, it cannot be abandoned. The House distinguished abandonment and extinguishment of existing use rights from abandonment of planning permission. Such use rights are not in the nature of a permission, and abandonment means that they cease to be existing rights.

[Special provisions now apply to minerals permissions. Under Schedule 9 of the 1990 Act a prohibition order coupled with restoration conditions may be served in respect of operations which have permanently ceased (two years cessation with resumption unlikely). A suspension order may be served to protect the environment where operations have been temporarily suspended. There are special rules concerning discontinuance orders.]

(The House accepted that where two inconsistent planning permissions are granted, the implementation of one may render it physically impossible to carry out the other, as in *Pilkington v Secretary of State* (1974), see 2.1.3.)

Although planning permission cannot be abandoned, it is spent when it is implemented. Planning permission for a building is spent when the building is substantially complete. (For the meaning of completion, see *Sage v Secretary of State* (2003) at 4.2.1.) Planning permission for a material change of use is spent when the initial change takes place. The permission was not spent in *Pioneer Aggregates* – mining is a continuing activity and quarrying had not commenced on the southern part of the site.

Cynon Valley Borough Council v Secretary of State for Wales and Oi Mee Lam (1986)

Planning permission had been granted for a fish and chip shop. The use was then changed to an antique shop. It was contended, following *Pioneer Aggregates*, that the antique shop could revert back to a hot food shop because the planning permission for that use could not be abandoned.

The Court held that the permission was to change *from* use A *to* use B, not merely permission to use the property for use B for the indefinite future. Therefore the fish and chip shop permission was spent when it was implemented. If it were otherwise, such a planning permission would be indefinitely valid, and would resemble an 'unexploded bomb', liable to go off at any time when the owner chooses to revert to the use for which permission was given.

(Reversion to a hot food shop was permissible on a different ground.)

2.1.2 Development not in accordance with the permission

Where the development does not comply in a material respect with the planning permission, the development is unauthorised.

Handoll v Warner Goodman Streat (1995)

Planning permission was granted for the erection of a building, subject to an agricultural occupancy condition. The building was erected some 90 feet west of the approved location. The issue for the Court of Appeal was whether the agricultural occupancy condition applied to the building.

It was held that as the development was unauthorised, it was not subject to any conditions (and would be immune from enforcement after four years).

The Court overruled the Divisional Court in *Kerrier DC v Secretary of State for the Environment* (1980) where a bungalow erected with an unauthorised basement was held to be subject to the agricultural occupancy condition attached to the permission.

2.1.3 Multiple permissions

A planning permission cannot be implemented if, because of the implementation of another permission on the land, it has become physically impossible to do so in accordance with its terms.

Pilkington v Secretary of State for the Environment (1974)

The appellant acquired a strip of land of sufficient size for three houses with gardens. In 1954 he obtained planning permission for a bungalow in the middle of the strip with the whole of the site as its curtilage. A condition stated that the bungalow 'shall be the only dwelling to be erected' upon the strip of land. The bungalow was built. Subsequently the appellant discovered the existence of a permission granted in 1953. This permitted a bungalow to be built at the northern end of the strip and for the remainder of the land to be used as a smallholding.

The court held that what was authorised by the 1953 permission could not be implemented. It was no longer possible to build a bungalow ancillary to the smallholding which was to occupy the rest of the site. The existing bungalow had 'destroyed' the smallholding.

In determining whether an earlier permission is still valid, it is irrelevant that the carrying out of the permitted development might breach a condition attached to a later permission. The test is physical impossibility, not mere inconsistency or incompatibility.

Staffordshire County Council v NGR Land Developments Ltd and others (2002)

In 1956, planning permission was granted for the working of clay. In the course of clay working, a seam of coal was discovered which hindered further extraction of clay. So in 1987 planning permission was granted to the National Coal Board (NCB) for the extraction of the coal. The NCB acquired the rights to the relevant area, extracted coal by opencast working, and fully restored the area in accordance with the 1987 permission.

It was contended by the local planning authority that the clay working permission could no longer be implemented, as it would mean undoing all the work of reinstatement and aftercare in accordance with the conditions in the coal working permission.

The Court of Appeal held that the clay working permission was still valid. It was physically possible to carry out that permission according to its terms. The fact that it was incompatible with conditions in the coal permission was of no relevance.

2.1.4 Impact on private rights

The grant of planning permission does not authorise a private nuisance, nor does it supersede a restrictive covenant.

Hunter v Canary Wharf Ltd (1996)

Local residents brought actions in the tort of nuisance for interference with television reception caused by the

250-metre-high Canary Wharf tower. Canary Wharf Ltd submitted that the grant of planning permission authorised the construction and provided immunity from an action in nuisance. The Court of Appeal rejected this defence and the matter was not raised before the House of Lords. However, Lord Hoffmann reinforced the Court of Appeal's decision, saying:

'It would, I think, be wrong to allow the private rights of third parties to be taken away by a permission granted by the planning authority to the developer.'

(The interference was held not to be an actionable nuisance.)

Mortimer v Bailey (2004)

The respondents had the benefit of a restrictive covenant which provided that no alterations could be carried out on the appellants' neighbouring property without the respondents' consent, such consent not to be unreasonably withheld. The appellants informed the respondents of their intention to build an extension. The respondents refused consent on the grounds of light reduction, loss of winter sun, and loss of a view. Nevertheless, the appellants obtained planning permission and began work on the extension. It was held that the refusal of consent to the extension was reasonable. A mandatory injunction was awarded requiring the removal of the extension, as damages would not adequately compensate the respondents for the loss of the benefit of the covenant.

2.2 DURATION OF PLANNING PERMISSION

Section 91 provides that planning permission is granted subject to a condition that the development must be begun no later than three years from the date of the grant (or deemed grant) or such shorter or longer period as the authority directs.

Section 92 governs the duration of outline permission for building or other operations. Such permission is subject to a condition that application for approval of a reserved matter must be made not later than three years from the date of grant, and that the development must be begun no later than two years from the final approval of reserved matters or, in the case of approval on different dates, the final approval of the last such matter to be approved.

If development is not begun by the end of the relevant period, it is no longer authorised: section 93(4)(a).

2.2.1 Commencement of development

In relation to sections 91 and 92, section 56(3) provides that development is begun on the earliest date on which any 'material operation' comprised in the development begins to be carried out.

Material operation is further defined in section 56(4) to mean:

(a) 'any work of construction in the course of the erection of a building;

(aa) any work of demolition of a building;

(b) the digging of a trench which is to contain the foundations, or part of the foundations, of a building;

(c) the laying of any underground main or pipe to the foundations, or part of the foundations, of a building or to any such trench as is mentioned in paragraph (b);

(d) any operation in the course of laying out or constructing a road or part of a road;

(e) any change in the use of land which constitutes material development.'

In the context of the winning and working of minerals, development is taken to have begun on the earliest date on which any winning and working of minerals to which the relevant planning permission relates begins – *The Town and Country Planning (Minerals) Regulations* 1995.

Meaning of material operation

The word 'operation' does not have the restricted meaning attributed to operational development as something which results in a permanent physical change to the land. 'Operation' in the context of section 56 is given its ordinary and natural meaning.

Malvern Hills District Council v Secretary of State for the Environment (1982)

The developer accurately marked out the line and width of the first 250 feet of road for an estate of 25 houses. He used pegs which were 2.5 feet long by about 2 inches square and driven into the ground. The question for the Court of Appeal was whether the pegging out was within the definition of a 'specified operation' (now 'material operation' under the 1990 Act) as an 'operation in the course of laying out or constructing a road or part of a road'. The Court rejected the council's claim that operation bore the same meaning as 'operations' in the definition of development. The inspector's view, that 'laying out' was marking out the road on the ground in accordance with an approved plan as a necessary preliminary to construction of the road, was accepted by the Court.

Developer's intention of no relevance

There is no requirement for an intention by the developer to carry out or complete the development. If it were otherwise it would create uncertainty.

East Dunbartonshire Council v Secretary of State for Scotland (1999)

Lord Coulsfield, delivering the judgment of the Court of Session, Inner House, considered all the authorities and said:

> '... there is no justification in the terms or in the structure of the legislation for the imposition of an ill-defined requirement that the specified operations should be carried out with some particular intention. In our view, the proper test is an objective one ...'

Riordan Communications Ltd v South Buckingham District Council (2000)

Building work was delayed because of the owner's financial difficulties, but a few days before the time limit expired, some demolition and foundation work was undertaken to avoid the lapse of permission. The local planning authority claimed that the permission had lapsed because at the time of the initial work the developer had no genuine intention to carry out the development.

The judge held, following the *East Dunbartonshire Council* case, that there is nothing in the 1990 Act to indicate the requirement of an intention. It is simply a question of fact and degree whether the works were done in accordance with the permission and whether they were material in the sense of not being *de minimis* (trifling).

Operations in breach

Work done in breach of a planning condition will not normally constitute commencement of development. But this rule has to be applied with common sense, so the courts have allowed exceptions in certain cases.

Whitley & Sons v Secretary of State for Wales and Clwyd County Council (1992)

Planning permission was granted for the extraction of minerals subject to conditions about restoration, landscaping and a scheme of working, all of which reserved matters had to be agreed with the local planning authority (or, failing agreement, the Secretary of State) before working started. Development had to be begun by 30 November 1978. The developer made an application for approval of the reserved matters in July 1977. It was not until October 1978 that a decision was made by the planning committee – a rejection of the developer's proposals. This gave the developer about a month to obtain approval from the Secretary of State – a practical impossibility. The developer thus felt he had no alternative but to attempt to begin the development by commencing mining operations by 30 November. These works were limited and ended in early December. The Secretary of State approved the reserved matters in May 1982 and work in accordance with this approval commenced in September 1983. The local authority then took enforcement action claiming that the planning permission had not been validly implemented within the time limit.

Lord Justice Woolf confirmed the general rule that an operation in breach of condition cannot properly be described as commencing the development authorised by the permission. In this case, however, application for approval had been made within the time limits, that approval had eventually been given, and the operations were now immune from enforcement action (four years having elapsed). In these circumstances the permission had been validly implemented. The same would be true if, although the operations were not immune, approval had been obtained prior to enforcement action.

An exception may be made where the breach is purely technical and the developer has complied with the condition in substance.

R v Flintshire County Council, ex parte Somerfield Stores Ltd (1998)

A planning condition required a study of the report on the highway effects of the development to be submitted for approval before development commenced. It was claimed that this condition was not complied with before development commenced, as there was no record of an application for approval and no record of a decision.

The court held that the condition had been complied with in substance. All that was missing was the formality of a written application and written notice of approval. The work had been in conformity with the approved plans with the full knowledge and co-operation of the planning and highway authorities. It would have been unreasonable for the council to have decided that the permission could not be implemented.

Commencing building operations before the resolution of all reserved matters or full compliance with pre-conditions has risks, even if it is acceptable to the local planning authority. This is because:

(a) the start of building operations in breach does not count as commencement of development, so the planning permission will lapse if the conditions are not complied with in time;

(b) the informal waiver of conditions is not valid – a condition can only be lifted by application under section 73 (see 3.4.5).

Henry Boot Homes Ltd v Bassetlaw District Council (2002)

The appellant purchased land which had outline planning permission for housing. Some houses were built before all of the pre-conditions were complied with. It then transpired that the planning permission may have been obtained by corruption and so the local authority were considering revoking or modifying the permission in respect of part of the land that the (innocent) appellant had purchased. However, the authority confirmed that they considered the appellant's permission to be valid and indicated that the permission had been implemented. Negotiations ensued and the appellant was invited to make a new planning application for a revised scheme. A third party threatened judicial review if this was granted, and so the local authority reminded the appellant about the need to comply with the conditions. Eventually the time limit expired before all the conditions were complied with and it was contended that the permission had lapsed.

The appellant claimed that it had a 'legitimate expectation' that the local authority would treat the development as having commenced before the time limit had expired because it had indicated that planning permission had been implemented. It also claimed that the authority had power to waive compliance with conditions. The Court of Appeal held that the scope for waiver by non-statutory means must be 'very limited' now that section 73 provides a statutory procedure engaging the public. For similar reasons, legitimate expectation will only arise in exceptional circumstances because cases where there is no third party or public interest in a planning decision will be very rare. In the circumstances, no legitimate expectation arose.

2.2.2 Revocation and modification orders

Section 97 gives a local planning authority power to revoke or modify a planning permission if it is expedient to do so. Section 100 provides the Secretary of State with a similar power. The power can only be exercised before operations have been completed or before a change of use has taken place.

The fact that a local planning authority will have to pay compensation (under section 107) if a revocation or modification order is made is not a material consideration.

Alnwick District Council v Secretary of State for the Environment (1999)

Alnwick District Council had granted outline planning permission for up to 4,654 square metres of class A1 use, mistakenly believing they were granting permission for 3,252 square metres. The Secretary of State modified the permission by deleting the class A1 use. This would result in Safeway having a claim for compensation from the Council in excess of £4m and would mean that a planned leisure facility could not go ahead. The Council claimed that the inspector, on whose report the Secretary of State's decision was based, had erred in law in disregarding the financial consequences of making the order. The court rejected this claim. The compensation is not a land use planning matter.

Compensation is due to any person 'interested in the land'. This includes a licensee with a substantial right in the land.

Pennine Raceway v Kirklees Metropolitan Borough Council (1982)

The appellant had what amounted to a yearly licence to promote motor vehicle and motor cycle events on an old airfield. The licensee had spent a considerable amount of money on landscaping and car parking. The Court of Appeal held that 'interested in the land' in this context does not mean merely having a legal interest in the land. A substantial right, such as this licence, entitled the appellant to compensation.

2.2.3 Discontinuance orders

Section 102 gives a local planning authority power to require the discontinuance of any use, impose conditions on the continuance of any use, and require the removal of buildings or works. Compensation is then due for the loss of the rights. Mining operations are treated as a 'use' for this purpose under Schedule 9.

Parkes v Secretary of State for the Environment (1979)

A discontinuance order required the cessation of the use of land for storing and processing of scrap. The appellant claimed that, as storing and processing were operations, he was not carrying out a use.

The Court of Appeal disagreed. Operations in this context means physical alteration to the land with some degree of permanence. So the storing and processing was a use.

2.3 OUTLINE PLANNING PERMISSION

An outline planning permission may be obtained for the erection, alteration or extension of a building. The effect is to grant consent subject to a condition requiring the approval of those 'reserved matters' which are not detailed in the application: article 1(2) of the *Town and Country Planning (General Development Procedure) Order* 1995. 'Reserved matters' are defined in article 1(2) as:

(a) 'siting,

(b) design,

(c) external appearance,

(d) means of access,

(e) the landscaping of the site.'

[The Secretary of State is empowered by the *Planning and Compulsory Purchase Act* 2004 to make regulations requiring further details to be submitted with outline planning applications in the form of design and access statements. At the time of writing he is consulting on the form of these statements.]

The scale of development is not a 'reserved matter' within article 1(2) as it does not fall within 'siting' or 'design'. So limitations on floorspace or density should be dealt with by an appropriate condition on the grant of permission.

It is not possible to reserve matters of which details have been given in the outline application (unless the details were included 'for illustrative purposes only'). The planning authority may seek further details (article 3(2)) but the applicant may appeal to the Secretary of State if he does not wish to comply.

R v Newbury District Council, ex parte Chieveley Parish Council (1999)

Newbury and District Agricultural Society submitted an application for outline permission including details as to siting and means of access. Outline permission was granted subject to a condition that:

'full details of the siting, design and external appearance of the building(s) and other works, the means of access thereto, and the landscaping of the site (the "reserved matters") shall be submitted to the Local Planning Authority not later than ...'

The Court of Appeal held that this condition was unlawful as it purported to reserve matters of which details had been given in the outline application.

The Court also observed that the scale or quantum of development cannot be brought within the words 'siting' or 'design'. So if the authority wishes to limit floorspace, for example, it must not regard it as one of the 'reserved matters' but should attach an appropriate condition. If the outline application specifies the floor area then, unless it is refused or withdrawn, it commits those concerned to a development on that scale 'subject to minimal changes and to such adjustments as can reasonably be attributed to siting, design and external appearance'.

2.3.1 Application for approval of reserved matters

An application for approval of reserved matters must be within the terms of the outline permission. So long as this is the case the developer may make different applications in respect of the same part, or make applications for separate parts of the development.

Heron Corporation Ltd v Manchester City Council (1978)

Heron Corporation were granted outline permission for the comprehensive redevelopment of an eight acre site in Manchester. After an application for reserved matters for phase 1 of the development was granted, a number of buildings within the site were listed and could no longer be demolished. So Heron submitted an application for a new layout which retained the listed buildings. The local planning authority contended that, once reserved matters have been approved, they cannot be revised or varied by a further submission of reserved matters under the same outline consent.

The Court of Appeal disagreed. Lord Denning MR said that he could see no reason why the applicant should not make another and different application for approval. Likewise he saw no reason why the application for approval of a reserved matter should cover the whole site.

'When a big development is in progress, when it is done in stages or phases, an application can be made for approval of the plans for each part or phase in time, without the developer committing himself to the details of a later stage or phase.'

An application for approval of reserved matters cannot be refused if this would, in effect, revoke or modify the grant of permission.

Proberun Ltd v Secretary of State for the Environment (1990)

The Secretary of State, on appeal, had granted outline permission for 90 holiday homes. One of the reserved matters was approval for the means of access to the site. The highway authority required the junction between the access road and the main road to be reconstructed or the access road to be moved to emerge at a different point. Either of these would necessitate the acquisition of land not in the control of the developer. The local planning authority failed to make a decision within the time limit and the developer appealed. The inspector quashed the appeal on the ground of the unsuitability of access and the developer challenged that decision in the courts.

The Court of Appeal held that, as the developer's proposals, although unsatisfactory, were the best that could be achieved within the limits of the site, to refuse permission would be a misuse of power. It would achieve, without compensation, a revocation or modification order.

Permission will lapse if no complete application for reserved matters is made within the time limit specified.

Coghurst Wood Leisure Park Ltd v Secretary of State for Transport, Local Government and the Regions (2002)

Outline planning permission was granted for 250 holiday chalets. Shortly before expiry of the time limit an application was made for reserved matters. This application showed the siting of only 18 chalets and stated that the siting of the remainder would be determined during construction. Approval was granted for the reserved matters. Subsequently, the court determined that the outline planning permission had lapsed. The application must include 'such particulars and be accompanied by such plans and drawings as are necessary to deal with matters reserved' (now article 4 of the *Town and Country Planning (General Development Procedure) Order* 1995) and so it was invalid.

2.4 INTERPRETATION OF PLANNING PERMISSION

In construing an unambiguous planning permission, regard may be had only to the permission itself. So the planning application or other documents must be disregarded unless they are expressly incorporated by reference into the permission.

Miller-Mead v Minister of Housing and Local Government (1963)

Land had existing use rights for parking caravans for repair, storage and display for sale. In 1954 an application was made for planning permission to continue this use. Temporary permission was granted for 'parking of caravans' on the site, expiring on 31 December 1956. In 1955 the owner began to use the land for residential caravans. Enforcement action was taken on 28 December 1960. If the permission was just for storage of caravans, the unlawful residential use would have been in excess of four years and immune. If, on the other hand, the permission was for residential use, it would not be. So the owner contended that the permission should be read with the application and was limited to storage.

The Court of Appeal disagreed. A grant of permission runs with the land and a successor in title is entitled to rely on the actual words of the grant. 'Parking of caravans' implies no restriction on the use of those caravans, so residential use was permitted.

If there is ambiguity in the permission it is permissible to look at extrinsic material, including the application, to resolve it.

R v Ashford Borough Council, ex parte Shepway District Council (1999)

In this case Mr Justice Keene set out the legal principles applicable to the use of extrinsic material in construing a planning permission. He observed that when recourse is had to the planning application in resolving a particular ambiguity in the permission, this does not mean that the whole application is thereby incorporated into the permission. That would be contrary to the rule in *Miller-Mead*.

Where there is a discrepancy between the permission and the application, this does not affect the construction of the permission if it is plain on its face. However, there is a possibility that a permission which is substantially greater than the application may be invalid. If so, it must be challenged promptly.

R v Secretary of State for the Environment, ex parte Slough Borough Council (1995)

The local authority applied for outline permission for land it owned with a view to subsequent disposal. The application sought permission for the erection of office buildings with a specified floorspace of 1,055 square metres. In the subsequent grant of permission, there were the usual conditions about approval of reserved matters, but no reference to floorspace whatsoever. The land was sold and the new owner's application for approval of reserved matters stated that the proposed floorspace would be 1,530 square metres. The council refused to approve this application and the owner appealed. The issue was whether the application was within the terms of the outline permission. It was held that it was.

Lord Justice Stuart-Smith said:

'It should be borne in mind that breach of a planning permission may lead to criminal sanctions. The public should be able to rely on a document that is plain on its face without being required to consider whether there is any discrepancy between the permission and the application.'

The Court said that the size of the development may properly be reduced having regard to the reserved matters such as siting, design, landscaping and access. (Note that the scope of this reduction is 'minimal' according to the Court of Appeal in *R v Newbury District Council*, above.)

The Court observed that if a planning permission is substantially greater than the application then it might be invalid, as those who might have objected to it have been denied that opportunity (approving *Bernard Wheatcroft Ltd v Secretary of State for the Environment* (1981) on this point). However, a challenge to validity must be made promptly, and in this case had long since passed.

2.5 PLANNING DECISIONS

The *Town and Country Planning (General Development Procedure) Order* 1995 sets out the procedure for dealing with a planning application (such as publicity, consultation, etc.). Article 22 requires that the decision notice shall include a summary of reasons and relevant policies when granting permission, and provide full reasons and all relevant policies when refusing permission or imposing conditions.

R (on the application of Wall) v Brighton and Hove City Council (2004)

The planning authority failed to give the summary of reasons for the grant of permission. A neighbour sought judicial review and planning officers sought to remedy the defect by asking members to state their reasons and summarising those reasons in an amended notice of grant.

Although the case was 'finely balanced', the High Court exercised its discretion to quash the decision to grant planning permission. The applicant suffered from the uncertainty and delay, although she was not substantially prejudiced, and in the circumstances the error was not adequately remedied by obtaining the reasons by correspondence some five months after the decision.

2.6 PLANNING APPEALS – SECTION 78

Section 78 establishes a right to appeal against planning decisions of the local planning authority, including the failure to take such decisions within a specified period (deemed refusal). It covers both refusal and conditional grant whether in respect of outline or detailed permission or in respect of approval required by a development order.

2.6.1 Powers of the Secretary of State

The Secretary of State may allow or dismiss the appeal, reverse or vary any part of the decision (whether the appeal relates to that part or not) and deal with the application as if made to him in the first instance.

Transferred jurisdiction

The Secretary of State's jurisdiction is transferred to appointed persons (the planning inspectorate) except for operational land of statutory undertakers, but he may recover jurisdiction in accordance with certain published criteria.

2.6.2 The appeal process

An appeal may be by way of written representations if the appellant and local planning authority waive their right to appear before an inspector – section 79(2).

A hearing is less formal than a public local inquiry and the inspector leads a discussion about the issues. This does not alter the fact that a fair and thorough examination of the issues is required.

Dyason v Secretary of State for the Environment, Transport and the Regions (No. 1) (1998)

The Court of Appeal held that the absence of formal cross-examination created a danger that propositions were not thoroughly examined and that the inspector, possibly put off guard by the relaxed formality, did not provide the fair hearing required. There was insufficient inquiry into the agricultural justification of a large building for ostrich breeding. A hearing imposes an inquisitorial duty on the inspector to thoroughly investigate and examine the issues. Any suggestion that the requirements of a hearing are fundamentally different from a public inquiry is to be resisted.

2.6.3 Burden of proof

The concept 'burden of proof' is not appropriate to planning appeals.

J A Pye (Oxford) Estates Ltd v West Oxfordshire District Council and the Secretary of State for the Environment (1982)

The judge rejected the appellant's claim that a burden of proof lay upon the local planning authority. He stated that the local planning authority will put forward what they consider to be sound and clear-cut planning reasons for refusal. The inquiry then inevitably takes the form of the appellant challenging the grounds and the authority defending them, but this should not lead to a comparison with civil litigation. The inspector's task is to consider the facts and contentions and determine whether there are any sound and clear-cut reasons for refusal. There is nothing objectionable in the inspector using such phrases as 'I am not satisfied that such a point has been made out', 'provided it is clear that it is in this overall context'.

2.6.4 Reasons for the decision

There is a duty under the *Town and Country Planning (Inquiries Procedure) (England) Rules* 2000 to give reasons for the decision in a public local inquiry. Reasons must be proper, adequate, intelligible and deal with the substantial points that have been raised.

Hope v Secretary of State for the Environment (1975)

'It seems to me that the decision must be such that it enables the appellant to understand on what grounds the appeal has been decided and be in sufficient detail to enable him to know what conclusions the inspector has reached on the principal important controversial issues.' (Mr Justice Phillips, approved by the House of Lords in *Save Britain's Heritage v Number 1 Poultry Ltd* (1991))

The degree of particularity required depends entirely on the nature of the issues falling for decision (Lord Bridge in *Save*

Britain's Heritage). The decision maker does not have to mention every material consideration, so long as he has had regard to them and has dealt with the controversial issues.

Save Britain's Heritage v Number 1 Poultry Ltd (1991)

'In so far as he was saying that a decision letter must refer to each material consideration I must respectfully disagree ... What the Secretary of State must do is to state his reasons in sufficient detail to enable the reader to know what conclusion he has reached on the "principal important controversial issues".' (Lord Lloyd)

There is a statutory duty to provide reasons in hearings, but not in written representations cases. However, a request for reasons is implicit.

North Wiltshire District Council v Secretary of State for the Environment and Clover (1992)

The Court of Appeal held that, as reasons have in practice invariably been given on the written representations procedure, in that circumstance a request is implicit in the acceptance of that procedure.

Where the inspector's reasons do not indicate whether he has had regard to a material consideration which was placed before him (in this case an earlier appeal decision) there must usually be substantial doubt whether the decision taken was within the powers of the 1990 Act. In that circumstance the interests of an applicant will have been substantially prejudiced by the deficiency of reasons, for he is left in doubt as to his ability to challenge on that ground.

2.6.5 Costs

The Secretary of State has discretion to award costs under section 250(5) of the *Local Government Act* 1972 in respect of an inquiry or a hearing. Costs will be awarded against a party who has behaved unreasonably. See the guidance in Circular 8/93.

P & O Developments Ltd v Secretary of State for the Environment (1990)

The Secretary of State awarded costs against the applicants for an appeal against the refusal of a large retail and leisure centre in the green belt. The applicants challenged this decision on the basis that, although there was a strong green belt presumption against such schemes, there were special circumstances in this case. The court held that the Secretary of State was entitled to find that the appellants had no reasonable prospect of success and so his discretion to award costs could not be interfered with.

2.6.6 Third parties

Third parties have no right to lodge a planning appeal against a local planning authority decision, but if they have *locus standi* or are 'persons aggrieved' they may be able to challenge the decision of a local planning authority or the Secretary of State in the High Court on a point of law, below.

2.7 CHALLENGING PLANNING DECISIONS IN THE COURTS

Some decisions of the local planning authority may be challenged in the High Court by way of judicial review. Decisions of the Secretary of State are subject to a statutory right of challenge in the High Court.

In rare cases, a person may be able to bring a private law action for damages where that does not involve a public law issue. See, for example, *Davy v Spelthorne Borough Council* (1984) where the claimant sought damages in the tort of negligence.

2.7.1 Judicial review

Various provisions of the 1990 Act (below) preclude the right to legal challenge of planning decisions, except in accordance with the Act. However, they do not apply to decisions of local planning authorities in determining planning applications. A person with *locus standi* may claim judicial review in the High Court and seek a mandatory order, a prohibiting order, a quashing order, or an injunction. A person may also seek a declaration as to the law. The remedies are discretionary and the court may refuse to grant relief in appropriate circumstances.

2.7.1.1 Grounds of challenge

These include *ultra vires*, error of law, *Wednesbury* unreasonableness, ignoring a material consideration, taking account of an immaterial consideration, and breach of the rules of natural justice. Illustrations of these may be seen in many of the cases on planning conditions, planning obligations and material considerations in Chapter 3. *Wednesbury* unreasonableness derives from *Associated Provincial Picture Houses v Wednesbury Corporation* (1947) and means a decision so manifestly or obviously unreasonable that no reasonable decision maker could have arrived at it. It includes such things as perversity and irrationality.

Natural justice or procedural fairness

Natural justice requires that a person is treated fairly and has the opportunity of putting his case (see the *Fairmount Investments* case, at 2.7.2.3). It also requires the absence of bias or predetermination.

Bias and predetermination

If a decision maker has a personal interest in the outcome of a decision, then the decision must be set aside. If he has no personal interest, but the decision maker's conduct indicates partisanship or prejudgment such that there is a real possibility of bias, the decision will be set aside.

R (on the application of Ghadami) v Harlow District Council (2004)

The claimant sought judicial review of a resolution by the Harlow planning committee to grant permission for a major redevelopment of a retail centre. From telephone conversations recorded and transcribed by the claimant it appeared that the chairman of the planning committee was anxious to see the proposed development take place and was seeking to remove the potential blockage or delay that the claimant could cause. In the circumstances, there was a real possibility that the chairman was biased in the sense of approaching the decision with a closed mind and without impartial consideration of all relevant planning issues. As the permission was granted by such a narrow majority, the decision should be quashed.

2.7.1.2 Locus standi

The applicant must have sufficient standing to challenge a planning decision and must not be a mere busybody. Traditionally the courts have distinguished between members of the public generally and a person who has a particular interest, although recently the judicial approach has been more liberal in the case of pressure groups or even public spirited taxpayers.

R v North Hertfordshire District Council, ex parte Sullivan (1981)

A neighbour who had objected to a decision that would intrude upon her privacy was held to have locus standi.

R v Canterbury City Council, ex parte Springimage Ltd (1993)

A landowner whose prospects of obtaining planning permission were likely to be adversely affected by the decision had locus standi.

R v Sheffield City Council, ex parte Power (1994)

An unincorporated association of local residents who wished to challenge the grant of an established use certificate had locus standi.

R v Inspectorate of Pollution and another, ex parte Greenpeace (No. 2) (1994)

The case concerned the new THORP plant at Sellafield. Greenpeace had been treated as a consultee and was not an officious bystander or busybody. It had 4,500 members in Cumbria and could provide the resources and expertise that individual employees or neighbours could not.

R (on the application of Kides) v South Cambridgeshire District Council (2001)

A long-standing resident of a village sought to challenge the grant of permission for a large housing development nearby. She was opposed to any housing whatsoever, but based on her challenge on matters in which she had no personal interest, such as the alleged failure to consider new policies on affordable housing.

Nevertheless the Court of Appeal were of the opinion that she was not a mere meddler but had a real and genuine interest in seeking to prevent substantial development and must be able to present her challenge on all available grounds.

2.7.1.3 Time limit

The procedural rules for claiming judicial review state that the claim must be filed promptly and in any event not later than three months after the grounds to make the claim first arose. The interpretation of these rules was examined by the House of Lords in the *Burkett* case.

R v London Borough of Hammersmith and Fulham, ex parte Burkett (2002)

The House of Lords held that the time runs from the date that planning permission is granted, not the date of the resolution to grant planning permission, as had formerly been held to be the case.

As regards the time limit, the House criticised an earlier decision of the High Court that purported to reduce the time limit to six weeks in line with the time limit on statutory challenge. Furthermore, the House doubted that the word 'promptly' was sufficiently certain in meaning to comply with European law and Convention rights. However, the court has discretion to refuse relief and in urgent cases the burden to act quickly would be on the applicant.

2.7.2 Statutory challenge to a decision made under section 78

Section 79(5) provides that the determination of the Secretary of State on a planning appeal shall be final. Nevertheless, sections 284 and 288 allow a challenge on legal grounds in the courts. Section 284 states that, except as provided in the 1990 Act, any decision on an appeal under section 78 shall not be challenged in any legal proceedings whatsoever. Section 288 provides that persons aggrieved by a decision of the Secretary of State may apply to the High Court to question its validity on grounds of ultra vires.

2.7.2.1 Who may challenge under section 288

A 'person aggrieved' may apply to the High Court under section 288. A person aggrieved includes a third party who is, in the ordinary sense of the word, aggrieved by the decision.

Turner v Secretary of State for the Environment (1973)

'Person aggrieved' does not have a restricted meaning as some early authorities suggested.

> '... any person who, in the ordinary sense of the word is aggrieved by the decision, and certainly any person who has attended and made representations at the inquiry, should have the right to establish in the courts that the decision is bad in law ...' (Mr Justice Ackner)

Times Investment Ltd v Secretary of State for the Environment and Tower Hamlets London Borough Council (1990)

The Court of Appeal upheld the approach in *Turner* and held that a person who purchased the appellant's land was a person aggrieved by the decision of the Secretary of State. (The purchase was made after the appeal and before the decision.)

2.7.2.2 Grounds for challenge – section 288(1)

A challenge to an order or action of the Secretary of State may be made on the grounds:

(i)   that it is not within the powers of the 1990 Act; or

(ii)   that any of the relevant requirements have not been complied with in relation to it.

Ground (i) – substantive ultra vires

The judicial interpretation of 'not within the powers' means ultra vires in its broadest sense, not just that the decision, on the face of it, goes beyond the powers of the 1990 Act. The definition given by Lord Denning in the *Ashbridge* case, where he likened it to a challenge by way of judicial review, is normally cited.

Ashbridge Investments v Minister of Housing and Local Government (1965)

A minister's decision to include a house within a compulsory purchase order was challenged on the ground that it was not within his powers in the *Housing Act* 1957. Lord Denning said:

> 'Under this section it seems to me that the court can interfere with the Minister's decision if he has acted on no evidence; or if he has come to a conclusion to which on the evidence he could not reasonably come; or if he has given a wrong interpretation to the words of the statute; or if he has taken into consideration matters which he ought not to have taken into account, or vice versa. It is identical with the position when the Court has power to interfere with the decision of a lower tribunal which has erred in point of law.'

Section 288(5)(b) provides that the High Court 'may' quash the order or action if it is not within the powers of the 1990 Act. According to the Court of Appeal in *Bolton Metropolitan Borough Council v Secretary of State for the Environment* (1991) the discretion not to quash can be exercised in exceptional circumstances. In the *Berkeley* case the House of Lords indicated that the discretion is even more limited where there is non-compliance with an EU directive. (The relevant directive was Council Directive 85/337/EEC on environmental assessment.)

R v Secretary of State for the Environment, ex parte Berkeley (2000)

The Secretary of State granted permission for the redevelopment of Fulham FC's ground. His decision was challenged on the ground that no environmental impact assessment had been made. Counsel for the Secretary of State contended that the decision should stand because there was, in substance, compliance with the environmental assessment regulations, as the required environmental statement was to be found in the applicant's statement of case, together with the planning authority's statement of case to the inspector (which incorporated various background papers including letters from consultees).

Giving the judgment of the House of Lords, Lord Hoffman stated that this 'paper chase' could not be treated as the equivalent of an environmental statement. He held that there was a failure to comply with the legislation and doubted that the court could exercise a discretion to uphold a planning permission that has been granted contrary to the terms of a directive. It might be different if there was a failure to observe the requirements of a clearly superfluous procedural step.

Ground (ii) – procedural ultra vires

This ground is subject to the provision in section 288(5)(b) that the interests of the applicant have been substantially prejudiced.

2.7.2.3   General principles of review in planning appeals – the Seddon Properties case

Mr Justice Forbes in *Seddon Properties Ltd v Secretary of State for the Environment* (1978) helpfully summarised the main principles under which a decision of the Secretary of State in a planning appeal can be challenged in the High Court.

Seddon Properties Ltd v Secretary of State for the Environment and Macclesfield Borough Council (1978)

The Seddon principles:

- The Secretary of State must not act perversely. This is another example of the *Wednesbury* principle.
- The Secretary of State must not take account of irrelevant material or fail to take into account that which is relevant (*Ashbridge Investments Ltd v Minister of Housing and Local Government*).

- The Secretary of State must abide by the statutory procedures, in particular the inquiries procedure rules [now the 2000 Rules]. These rules require him to give reasons for his decision after a planning inquiry and those reasons must be proper and adequate reasons which are clear and intelligible and deal with the substantial points which have been raised.

- The Secretary of State must not depart from the principles of natural justice – Lord Justice Russell in *Fairmount Investments v Secretary of State for the Environment* (1976), below.

- If the Secretary of State differs from his inspector on a finding of fact or takes into account any new evidence or issue of fact not canvassed at the inquiry he must, if this involves disagreeing with his inspector's recommendations, notify the parties and give them at least an opportunity of making further representations: Rule 12 of the *Town and Country Planning (Inquiries Procedure) (England) Rules* 2000.

Natural justice

If there is a breach of the principles of natural justice, then the action or order is not within the powers of the 1990 Act.

If the Secretary of State or an inspector bases his decision on a matter that was not raised at the inquiry, he will have denied a party the opportunity of challenging it.

Fairmount Investments v Secretary of State for the Environment (1976)

A compulsory purchase order was sought in respect of a number of houses which the local authority said were unfit for human habitation. Fairmount contested this and claimed that the houses could be rehabilitated. An inquiry was held and the inspector upheld the order on the ground that the foundations were inadequate and so the houses could not be rehabilitated. The question of the inadequacy of the foundations had not been raised by the local authority before or at the inquiry.

The House of Lords held that there had been a breach of the rules of natural justice. The appellants had not been given any opportunity to deal with the suggestion that the foundations were inadequate. The inspector should either have reconvened the hearing or, in a straightforward case like this, invited views on his provisional conclusions.

2.7.2.4 Time limit

The application must be made within six weeks from the date on which the order is confirmed or, as the case may be, the date on which the action is taken – section 288(3).

Time starts to run on the date the order is confirmed or the date on which the action is taken, not the time it is received.

Griffiths v Secretary of State for the Environment (1983)

The Secretary of State's decision letter was dated 8 December 1980 but was not received until 13 December. The application to the High Court was made on 22 January. The Secretary of State therefore contended that it was out of time. The appellant claimed that no person could be 'aggrieved' until he had notice of the decision, and so his application was not out of time.

The House of Lords held that the relevant action is taken on the date stamped on the decision letter. This is consistent with other statutory references to decision making as distinct from giving notice.

Six weeks is 42 days from the date of confirmation.

Okolo v Secretary of State for the Environment (1997)

The case concerned a challenge to a compulsory purchase order under the *Acquisition of Land Act* 1981. The application to court must be made within six weeks from the date on which the order is first published – a provision equivalent to the one in section 288 of the 1990 Act. It was held that this means that if the order were published on a Monday, the six weeks would begin on the next day (Tuesday) and expire at the end of the Monday in six weeks' time. The Tuesday following would be a day late. The corresponding date rule, applicable to months because of their different lengths, does not apply.

It has long been established that the time limit for applications to challenge orders of the Secretary of State, whether in highways, compulsory purchase, or planning, is absolute.

R v Secretary of State, ex parte Kent (1990)

Vodafone appealed against the refusal of planning permission for the erection of a 30 metre phone mast. There were blocks of flats nearby and the Secretary of State advised the local authority to immediately notify local residents so that they could make representations. Some residents were notified but many, including the applicant, were not. He claimed a breach of the rules of natural justice.

The Court of Appeal held (following *R v Secretary of State for the Environment, ex parte Ostler* (1976)) that for reasons of certainty and finality, the time limit is absolute and cannot be circumvented by claiming the decision is a nullity.

2.7.3 Right to a hearing by an independent tribunal – Article 6(1) of the European Convention on Human Rights

Article 6(1) provides that:

'In the determination of his civil rights and obligations or of any criminal charge against him, everyone is entitled to a fair and public hearing within a reasonable time by an independent and impartial tribunal established by law ...'

A planning inspector is not an independent and impartial tribunal, but the right to High Court review renders the planning process compliant with Article 6(1).

Bryan v United Kingdom (1996)

Mr Bryan appealed against an enforcement notice. The notice was upheld by an inspector and Bryan's appeal to the High Court was dismissed.

Bryan applied to the European Commission of Human Rights alleging a violation of Article 6(1) in that the inspector was not independent or impartial and the High Court review was insufficient to comply as the Court had no power to disturb the inspector's findings of fact.

It was held that the executive power of the Secretary of State to revoke an inspector's appointment at any time deprives the inspector of the requisite appearance of independence. However, the scope of the review of the Court was sufficient to comply. Even though it is restricted to points of law, the inspector's decision could be quashed if he had regard to irrelevant factors or disregarded relevant factors, or if the evidence was not capable of supporting a finding of fact, or if the decision was perverse or irrational.

R (on the application of Alconbury Developments Ltd) v Secretary of State for the Environment, Transport and the Regions (2001)

This case was concerned with appeal decisions of the Secretary of State as distinct from an inspector. The principal issue was whether there was compliance with Article 6(1).

The House of Lords held that the Secretary of State can be both a policy maker and a decision taker where the courts have jurisdiction to conduct a judicial review of the lawfulness and fairness of a decision. The remedy by way of judicial review ensures compliance with Article 6(1).

2.7.4 Legal challenges to other planning decisions

Section 284(3) and section 288 also permit legal challenge to decisions of the Secretary of State on appeals relating to lawful use or development certificates, advertisement consent appeals, listed building and conservation area consent appeals, and tree preservation order appeals.

For enforcement notice appeals, see Chapter 4.

2.8 THE GENERAL PERMITTED DEVELOPMENT ORDER 1995 ('GPDO')

Section 59 requires the Secretary of State to make a development order providing for the grant of planning permission. The order may grant permission itself or provide for the grant of permission by the local planning authority on an application in accordance with the order.

The GPDO grants permission to certain classes of development subject to certain conditions and limitations. It does not apply where the existing operations or use are unlawful.

2.8.1 Restrictions on the operation of the GPDO

Permitted development rights can be excluded by a special development order, an article 4 direction, an article 7 direction (certain minerals operations in designated areas), a planning condition, and an enforcement notice.

2.8.1.1 Article 4 directions

Article 4 of the GPDO provides that the Secretary of State or the appropriate local planning authority may give a direction that permitted development shall be prohibited in a specified area or that any particular permitted development shall be prohibited anywhere in the authority's area. The Secretary of State's approval is required for a local authority direction except in certain cases.

An article 4 direction can prohibit all or any development or prohibit a specific development.

Thanet District Council v Ninedrive Ltd (1978)

The defendants wished to hold a Sunday market on land at an old airfield. Class IV of the *General Development Order* 1977 ('GDO') permitted the use of land for markets for not more than 14 days in any calendar year. So the local planning authority made an order under article 4 removing this permitted development right in respect of the land at the airfield. Article 4 directions relating to Classes I–IV within a specified area did not require the Secretary of State's approval, but approval was needed to prohibit particular development. The defendants claimed that approval was required because the order was a direction that particular development should not be carried out.

Mr Justice Walton said:

'... the planning authority may either ban all or any development or ban a specific development, that is to say, it can either sweep the board clean or be as extremely selective as it chooses.'

The direction was clearly restricted to a particular area, so approval was not required.

Compensation for withdrawal of permitted development rights

Where permitted development rights have been withdrawn and an application for planning permission has been refused, compensation is due to 'a person interested in the land' who has incurred abortive expenditure or otherwise sustained loss or damage due to the revocation or modification – sections 108 and 107.

'A person interested in land' is not limited to a person with a proprietary interest in the land in the conveyancing sense. So it can include licensees. See *Pennine Raceway v Kirklees Metropolitan Borough Council* (1982), at 2.2.2, a case where an article 4 direction took away the right to race motor vehicles for 14 days in any calendar year.

2.8.1.2 Conditions restricting the operation of the GPDO

Article 3(4) provides that nothing in the GPDO permits development contrary to any condition imposed by a planning permission. So where a permission authorises a use or development to which the GPDO applies, the consequential permitted development rights can be restricted by condition (an exceptional course of action according to government policy). Such a condition must be clearly expressed.

Dunoon Developments v Secretary of State for the Environment (1992)

A condition provided that 'the use of the premises shall be limited to the display, sale and storage of new and used cars'. Subsequently the premises were used as an indoor market. An enforcement notice was served and the developer claimed the use was permitted by the GDO 1988 – a change from sale of motor vehicles to class A1 (shops).

It was held that the condition was not specific enough to exclude the operation of the GDO. Clear words such as 'and no other purpose' as in *City of London Corporation v Secretary of State for the Environment* (1971) are required.

(Note that the change from car showroom to A1 is no longer permitted development.)

2.8.2 Permitted development

This section looks at a selection of classes of permitted development under Schedule 2 of the GPDO which have given rise to case law of some practical significance, principally in the residential field. Other parts and classes are omitted.

It should be noted that there are restrictions on the application of certain classes of permitted development in sensitive areas – the National Parks, areas of outstanding natural beauty, the Broads and conservation areas.

2.8.2.1 Part 1 – Development within the curtilage of a dwellinghouse

For the meaning of 'curtilage' see 1.7.9.1.

Tolerances

Development is not permitted unless it falls within the relevant tolerances relating to volume, area, height, position, etc. So if the operation exceeds the permitted tolerances in the relevant class, the whole operation is unlawful, not merely the excess.

Garland v Minister of Housing and Local Government (1968)

The appellant constructed a building well in excess of the ten per cent increase in cubic content allowed under the GDO 1963. The local planning authority served an enforcement notice alleging development without planning permission and requiring the whole construction to be demolished. The appellant claimed that the tolerance was a 'limitation' and that the enforcement notice should have alleged a breach of limitation, not development without permission, and required him to reduce the size of the building to the ten per cent tolerance.

The Court of Appeal held that the tolerances were part of the definition of permitted development, not limitations, so the whole building was unlawful and could be required to be totally removed.

Since the *Garland* case, the legislation has been amended to give planning authorities the discretion to under-enforce, so they can serve a enforcement notice requiring compliance with the terms of the permitted development – section 173(4)(a).

Class A – The enlargement, improvement or other alteration of a dwellinghouse

Meaning of dwellinghouse

For the purposes of the GPDO, 'dwellinghouse' does not include a building containing one or more flats, or a flat contained within such a building – article 1(2). For the meaning of the word 'dwellinghouse' see *Gravesham Borough Council v Secretary of State for the Environment* (1984), at 1.7.9.1.

There must be a dwellinghouse in existence when the operations are carried out. And even if there is a dwellinghouse, 'enlargement, improvement and other alteration' does not include complete rebuilding.

Sainty v Minister of Housing and Local Government (1964)

The appellant proposed to demolish two old cottages and replace them with two new houses of different design as it was impossible to render them fit as they were.

The court held that this proposal was not permitted development as it was quite clear that a rebuilding was involved.

The building must be sufficiently intact and not merely the ruins of a dwelling.

Trustees of the Earl of Lichfield's Estate v Secretary of State for the Environment and Stafford Borough Council (1985)

A house ceased to be occupied in 1979 and suffered vandalism. The doors and windows were boarded up and all the internal domestic fittings removed. The interior was dilapidated. However, there was a septic tank available and a supply of water and electricity. The Secretary of State considered the building to be uninhabitable in its present condition and therefore not a dwellinghouse.

On appeal, Mr Justice O'Neill approved a wider test set out by the Secretary of State in *Oak Tree Cottage, Hope Mansell* (1978) that:

'... while it is felt the building need not necessarily be a dwellinghouse actually in habitation at the time, there must at all times remain on the land a structure sufficiently intact as to reasonably support the description of a dwellinghouse and not merely the ruins of a dwelling.'

The judge also stated that the use had not been abandoned and this was a strong indication that the building was a dwellinghouse.

Stone cladding and other facing material

Stone cladding and other cosmetic work may be regarded as improvement or alterations. Permitted development is not limited to structural features.

Bradford Metropolitan District Council v Secretary of State for the Environment (1978)

The local planning authority refused permission for facing two redbrick semi-detached houses with stone cladding. The local planning authority claimed that it was not permitted development as it projected 'beyond the forwardmost part of any wall of the original dwelling' in the wording of GDO 1977. Taking a common-sense approach, the judge regarded the wall as including windowsills and moulded surrounds. So although the cladding projected beyond the original brickwork, it did not project beyond the wall in this sense.

The judge also dismissed the local authority's claim that permitted development only included structural features, as distinct from cosmetic work.

(Note that the wording in the current GPDO uses the phrase 'nearer to the highway ... than the part of the original dwellinghouse nearest to that highway ...'.)

There is a specific exclusion of cladding with stone, artificial stone, timber, plastic or tiles in the sensitive areas. Forms of facing outside this list are permitted (so long as the relevant tolerances are observed).

Tower Hamlets LBC v Secretary of State for the Environment (1994)

The local planning authority took enforcement action in respect of cement and pebbledash rendering in a conservation area. The judge determined that stone cladding entailed the use of blocks, often quite thin, applied as a covering to a wall. So rendering followed by a dressing of stone chips was not within the words 'cladding with stone'.

Meaning of 'enlargement'

Enlargement is not restricted to an increase in the amount of internal enclosed space.

Richmond upon Thames London Borough Council v Secretary of State for the Environment and Neale (1991)

This case was concerned with what is now Class B of Part 1 of the GPDO, 'the enlargement of a dwellinghouse consisting of an addition or alteration to the roof'.

A parapet wall was erected around a flat roof. Such works could not fall within Class A as that excludes alterations to the roof. The local planning authority served an enforcement notice on the basis that the parapet was not an enlargement and so was not within Class B either.

The judge held that, as planning is concerned with external appearance, the parapet wall was an enlargement – it makes the building taller. He found support for this approach in the fact that calculations of cubic content are based on external measurements.

In order to come within the GPDO, works of enlargement must be effected before an enlargement by virtue of a planning permission.

Watts v Secretary of State for Transport, Local Government and the Regions (2002)

Watts obtained planning permission for side and rear extensions. At the same time as implementing this planning permission he undertook a roof extension under Class B (see below). The combined enlargement of both the planning permission and the extension under Class B would go beyond the permitted limit on cubic content, so the local authority served an enforcement notice in respect of the roof extension. Watts contended that, as the roof extension had been 'substantially completed' before the bulk of the works permitted by the specific grant of permission had been done, it was permitted development. The inspector treated the combined works as one operation thereby breaching the cubic content limits.

The court rejected this approach. It is a matter of the sequence of the works. It is a question of fact and degree whether the other works have reached a stage where they have a cubic content so as to be capable of being part of a 'resulting building' (in the words of the GPDO).

Class B – The enlargement of a dwellinghouse consisting of an addition or alteration to its roof (subject to certain tolerances)

For the meaning of enlargement see the *Richmond* case, above.

Development which results in any part of the dwellinghouse exceeding the height of the highest part of the roof is not permitted. Roof is taken to mean roof of the dwellinghouse as a whole.

Hammersmith and Fulham Council v Secretary of State for the Environment and Davison (1994)

Wrought iron railings, surmounted by a wooden trellis, had been erected around the perimeter of a flat roof. Access to the roof was provided by a metal staircase installed from the existing door in a mansard roof down to the flat roof. Class B does not permit development which results in any part of the dwellinghouse exceeding the height of the highest part of the roof. (There is a similar provision in Class A). So the main issue for the judge was whether the words 'highest part of the roof' refer to the roof of the dwellinghouse as a whole, or that part of the roof where the alterations were made. He held the former. He saw no reason to cut down the scope of the words for to do so would create difficulties where roofs were complex.

Class C – Any other alteration to the roof of a dwellinghouse

Development that would result in a material alteration to the shape of a dwellinghouse is excluded from Class C.

Shape means more than just external appearance. If it did not, Class C would be devoid of meaning, for work that does not materially affect exterior appearance is not development anyway – section 55(2)(a).

Hammersmith and Fulham Council v Secretary of State for the Environment and Davison (1994)

A metal staircase was installed from the existing door of a mansard roof slope down to the flat roof of a two-storey extension. Was the staircase permitted development within Class A or C?

The inspector had decided that it fell within Class A as an alteration to the dwellinghouse. It was contended in the High Court that, as it was fixed to the roof it fell outside Class A (Class A excludes alterations to the roof). The judge stated that this was a question of fact. The staircase is 'clearly different from the parapet wall in the *Richmond* case' (above) and, although it was possible that on the facts it might be an alteration to the roof, it was far from clear that it was. However, the judge did not have to decide that question because if it were an alteration to the roof, it fell within Class C anyway. 'Shape' of a dwellinghouse undoubtedly meant more than just external appearance, otherwise Class C could never apply, and he took the view that, in this case, the staircase could not be said to affect the shape of the dwellinghouse materially, or otherwise.

Class D – The erection or construction of a porch

The development permitted by Class D is subject to specified tolerances.

Class E – Building within the curtilage of a dwellinghouse

This permits any building or enclosure in the curtilage of a dwellinghouse required for a purpose incidental to the enjoyment of the dwellinghouse as such (subject to certain tolerances).

'Incidental to enjoyment' must involve an element of objective reasonableness, otherwise anything could be said to be enjoyed by the house owner. Furthermore, it cannot include a commercial purpose.

Emin v Secretary of State for the Environment and Mid Sussex County Council (1989)

'The fact that such a building had to be required for a purpose associated with the enjoyment of a dwellinghouse could not rest solely on the unrestrained whim of him who dwelt there but connoted some sense of reasonableness in all the circumstances of the particular case ...'. (Sir Graham Eyre QC)

Croydon London Borough Council v Gladden (1994)

The local planning authority sought an injunction to restrain Gladden from erecting various large replica items on and about his house in a personal battle with the council. An issue arose as to whether the erection of a large wooden replica of a Spitfire could be 'enjoyment of the dwellinghouse as such'. Following *Wallington v Secretary of State for Wales* (see 1.7.9.1) it was held that the personal pleasure Mr Gladden derived from putting one in the eye of the council is not enjoyment of the dwellinghouse as a dwellinghouse.

Thurrock Borough Council v Secretary of State for the Environment, Transport and the Regions (2002)

This case concerned the use of land for the taking off and landing of helicopters and light aircraft and for the storage of aircraft. One of the issues in the case was the alleged right of the landowner under Class E to erect an aircraft hangar on his very large rear garden. Although not deciding the point, Lord Justice Schiemann stated that 'a conclusion that an aircraft hangar is required for the purpose of a dwellinghouse as such is surprising'. Furthermore, he pointed out that Class E would not authorise the erection of a building used for commercial purposes even though it was also required for a purpose incidental to the enjoyment of the dwellinghouse as such.

2.8.2.2   Part 2 – Minor operations

Class A – Gates, fences, walls

The erection, construction, maintenance, improvement or alteration of a gate, fence, wall or other means of enclosure (subject to certain tolerances).

To come within this definition, a wall must have some function of enclosure.

Prengate Properties v Secretary of State for the Environment (1973)

Lord Widgery CJ said that the permission:

'would not extend to someone who places a free standing wall in the middle of his garden in circumstances in which the wall neither encloses nor plays any part in the enclosure of anything.'

Where a wall is erected as part of a larger engineering operation (a retaining wall, for example) then, even though the wall is an enclosure, it is not permitted under Class A as it is part of a development which goes beyond what is permitted by that class. However, if at the time of enforcement action a wall is not part of a larger operation, then it is within Class A, and it does not necessarily lose that status if it is subsequently used as a retaining wall.

Prengate Properties v Secretary of State for the Environment (1973)

The appellants built a wall surrounding half the perimeter of a house. The house was on a raised level. They began to import soil with a view to providing new terracing and with the intention of using the wall as a retaining wall for the additional soil. The local planning authority served an enforcement notice requiring the removal of the soil and the wall. At the date of the notice there was not sufficient soil for the wall to be acting as a retaining wall.

Lord Widgery CJ said that the situation must be examined at the date of the enforcement notice. At this date the wall had not been incorporated into a larger operation. Although the owner may have intended to incorporate it, his intention is not necessarily conclusive. So at the relevant time the wall was authorised.

Lord Widgery also observed that if an enclosing wall subsequently becomes a retaining wall, it does not lose its permitted development rights merely because it has some function of retaining the soil as well.

The words 'or other means of enclosure' are governed by the 'ejusdem generis' rule; i.e. where general words follow specific words, the meaning of the general words is limited to *things of the same kind* as the specific words. So other means of enclosure must be the same kind of thing as a gate, fence or wall.

South Oxfordshire District Council v Secretary of State for the Environment and Keene (1986)

One of the issues in this case was whether an earthen embankment creating a reservoir was within the definition 'gate, fence, wall or other means of enclosure'. Mr Justice McCullough stated that it would plainly not be a gate, fence or wall and in considering whether it was 'other means of enclosure', the Secretary of State should construe that phrase *ejusdem generis* with gate, fence or wall.

Highway restriction

Development is not permitted under Part 2, Class A if it is adjacent to a highway 'used by vehicular traffic' and its height exceeds one metre.

R (on the application of Nicholson) v First Secretary of State (2005)

The appellant raised the height of a wall adjacent to a lane which was a public footpath. The only vehicular traffic that could use the lane was that wishing to gain access to the appellant's farm holding, an adjacent house, and land adjoining the lane. The appellant contended that the one metre height limit did not apply because the lane was a highway limited to pedestrians.

Mr Justice Collins held that the purpose of the height restriction was one of safety. So the legislation was concerned with de facto use. He also held that the height of the wall must be measured from the ground level of the highway, not from the ground level of the land behind.

Class C – painting

The painting of the exterior of any building or work, except for advertisement, announcement or direction.

Windsor and Maidenhead Borough Council v Secretary of State for the Environment (1988)

In this case about the repainting of a listed building in deep pink with black detailing, Mr Justice Mann said:

> 'I would regard the painting or the repainting of the building as being an operation normally undertaken by a person carrying on business as a builder. Accordingly, and subject to the provisions of the permission granted by the *Town and Country Planning General Development Order* 1977 and subject also to the painting or repainting affecting the external appearance of the building ..., it would constitute "development".'

2.8.2.3   Part 3 – Certain changes of use

See 1.7.9.4.

2.8.2.4   Part 4 – Temporary buildings and uses

Class A

Buildings, structures, plant and machinery, etc. required for the duration of operations.

Class B

The use of any land for any purpose for not more than 28 days in total in any calendar year, subject to certain exceptions such as caravans. The 28-day limit is reduced to 14 days for markets and motor vehicle racing.

If a temporary use creates conditions which make it difficult or impossible to revert to the normal use between times, it will be a material change of use outside Class B.

RW Ramsey and JP Ramsey v Secretary of State for the Environment and Suffolk Coastal District Council (2002)

In the 1980s the claimant, without planning permission, carried out engineering operations on grazing land in order to create banks, depressions and jumps for a track for off-road vehicles. In 1998 the claimant applied for a lawful development certificate in respect of 'use of the agricultural land for the purpose of vehicular sports and leisure activities for a period not exceeding 28 days in any one year'. At first instance it was held that as there were permanent physical changes to the land in connection with the vehicular use, it should not be regarded as temporary or occasional. The Court of Appeal disagreed. As there would be a reversion to land for grazing sheep between off-road activities, the vehicular use was still temporary. However, the Court stated that if physical changes or activities render the land difficult or impossible to use for agriculture, then the use would no longer be temporary. Lord Justice Robert Walker observed that an intensively used off-road track which created extremely muddy conditions might, as a matter of fact, be incapable of reverting to agricultural use.

If a local planning authority consider that a use is permanent, they do not have to wait for the expiry of the 28 or 14-day period before taking enforcement action. The permission under the GPDO does not cover the inception of permanent use.

Tidswell v Secretary of State for the Environment and Thurrock Borough Council (1977)

Enforcement action was taken in respect of a Sunday market that had operated on nine Sundays. The applicant challenged the validity of the notice on the ground that there was no breach of planning control. It was held by the Divisional Court that it was not for the local planning authority to investigate to decide whether the developer could bring himself within some exemption. There was evidence that the use was permanent, so the authority were entitled to take the view that the there had been a material change of use.

2.8.2.5 Part 5 – Caravan sites

The use of land as a caravan site is permitted if it falls within paragraphs 2 to 10 of Schedule 1 of the *Caravan Sites and Control of Development Act* 1960. This includes accommodation of persons employed in building or engineering works on or adjacent to the land where the works are being carried out. Use within the curtilage of a dwellinghouse and incidental to the enjoyment of the house is excluded.

Hammond v Secretary of State for the Environment and Maldon District Council (1997)

The appellant used a caravan for accommodation whilst he undertook work on the erection of a dwelling. (A planning inspector had held that this accommodation use was permitted under the GPDO.) After the dwelling was built, the appellant's daughter lived in the caravan. The appellant contended that, as the use was still residential, no material change of use had occurred.

The Court of Appeal disagreed. If the land becomes used for a purpose not within the GPDO then, prima facie, development will have occurred. Therefore, in this case, the purpose of its presence on the land reverted to being a purpose for use as human habitation which was not protected by the GPDO and was alien to the permitted agricultural use of the land.

2.8.2.6 Part 24 – Phone masts

Class A provides certain permitted development rights to telecommunications code system operators.

A mast under 15 metres tall is permitted development subject to certain conditions. One of the conditions requires the developer to apply to the local planning authority for a determination as to whether the prior approval of the authority will be required for the siting and appearance of the development. The authority must advertise the proposal if it is contrary to the development plan. In essence, the development cannot commence until the developer is informed that no prior approval is required, or the developer is given approval within 56 days, or 56 days expire with no notification of any decision.

Where a local authority fails to notify a phone operator within the 56-day period that approval is needed, this may be a breach of the human rights of objectors. This may give rise to a claim for damages under the *Human Rights Act* 1998.

R (on the application of Nunn) v First Secretary of State and T-Mobile (UK) Ltd (2005)

The local authority resolved to refuse prior approval for T-Mobile's phone mast, but, by mistake, only notified T-Mobile after the expiry of the 56-day period. T-Mobile took the view that the mast was permitted development and erected it. N, a local resident, claimed that her human rights under Article 6 of the Convention had been violated as, having successfully made representations to the local authority, she would be precluded from a determination by an inspector as to the merits of those representations.

The Court of Appeal upheld the validity of the permitted development. The *Human Rights Act* 1998 did not allow the Court to take away T-Mobile's rights. However, N's Article 6 rights had been infringed by the local authority and not only could she take her case before the Ombudsman, but she may have a claim for damages under section 8 of the *Human Rights Act* 1998.

3
Determining planning applications

3.1 THE STATUTORY DUTIES

Town and Country Planning Act 1990, section 70(2)

'In dealing with an application for planning permission, the authority shall have regard to the provisions of the development plan, so far as material to the application, and to any other material considerations.'

Planning and Compulsory Purchase Act 2004, section 38(6)

'If regard is to be had to the development plan for the purpose of any determination to be made under the planning Acts the determination must be made in accordance with the plan unless material considerations indicate otherwise.'

3.2 MATERIAL CONSIDERATIONS

In order to carry out the duties under section 70 of the 1990 Act and section 38 of the *Planning and Compulsory Purchase Act* 2004, it is necessary for the authority to have regard to material considerations. What are material considerations? Mr Justice Cooke's definition in *Stringer v Minister of Housing and Local Government* has generally been accepted as the starting point.

Stringer v Minister of Housing and Local Government (1971)

'In principle, it seems to me that any consideration which relates to the use and development of land is capable of being a planning consideration. Whether a particular consideration falling within that broad class is material in any given case will depend on the circumstances.'

The House of Lords set out a similar test in the *Great Portland* case.

Great Portland Estates plc v Westminster City Council (1984)

'The test, therefore, of what is a material "consideration" in the preparation of plans or in the control of development ... is whether it serves a planning purpose ... And a planning purpose is one which relates to the character of the use of land.' (Lord Scarman)

Materiality

A consideration is material if it might cause the decision maker to reach a different conclusion.

Bolton Metropolitan Borough Council v Secretary of State for the Environment and Greater Manchester Waste Disposal Authority (1991)

'The decision maker ought to take into account a matter which might cause him to reach a different conclusion to that which he would reach if he did not take it into account. Such a matter is relevant to his decision making process. By the verb "might", I mean where there is a real possibility that he would reach a different conclusion if he did take that consideration into account.' (Lord Justice Glidewell)

3.2.1 Statutory and non-statutory considerations

There is a distinction between matters a decision maker must take into account because statute requires it, and those where the obligation to take into account arises from the nature of the decision and of the matter in question.

Bolton Metropolitan Borough Council v Secretary of State for the Environment and Greater Manchester Waste Disposal Authority (1991)

'If the validity of the decision is challenged on the ground that the decision maker failed to take into account [a non-statutory consideration] it is for the judge to decide whether it was a matter which the decision maker should have taken into account.' (Lord Justice Glidewell)

3.2.2 Legality and merits

Whether a consideration is material is ultimately a matter of law for the courts, whereas the weight to give a material consideration is a matter for the decision maker – the planning authority or the Secretary of State. The courts are only concerned with the legality of a planning decision, not its merits.

Tesco Stores Ltd v Secretary of State for the Environment and West Oxfordshire District Council (1995)

Lord Hoffman said:

'The law has always made a clear distinction between the question of whether something is a material consideration and the weight which it should be given. The former is a question of law and the latter is a question of planning judgment, which is entirely a matter for the planning authority. Provided that the planning authority has regard to all material considerations, it is at liberty (provided that it does not lapse into Wednesbury unreasonableness) to give them whatever weight the planning authority thinks or no weight at all.'

3.2.3 Some examples

Policy

Government policy is obviously a material consideration. Decision makers must take account of relevant policies in Planning Policy Statements, Planning Policy Guidance Notes, Minerals Planning Guidance Notes, government circulars and other policy documents.

In a dispute about the meaning of a government policy, it is for the court to determine what the words are capable of meaning.

R v Derbyshire County Council, ex parte Woods (1997)

The applicant claimed that Derbyshire County Council had failed to interpret a paragraph of Minerals Planning Guidance Note 3 ('MPG3') properly.

The Court of Appeal held that it is for the court to determine, as a matter of law, what the words are capable of meaning. Lord Justice Brooke said:

'If the decision maker attaches a meaning to the words they are not properly capable of bearing, then it will have made an error of law, and it will have failed properly to understand policy.'

He added that MPG3 is not a set of rules written by lawyers for lawyers. It is a Guidance Note and not to be read as if it contained the words of a statute.

(A similar approach is taken to development plans. See *Cranage Parish Council v First Secretary of State* (2004).)

Particular occupiers

Although private rights are not normally material, the impact of the development on the use of another may be a material consideration.

Stringer v Minister of Housing and Local Government (1971)

The case concerned proposed development which could interfere with the reception of the radio telescope at Jodrell Bank. The developer claimed that to refuse permission in the interests of the telescope was to protect rights of a private character, but that planning decisions should protect only the public interest in the sphere of amenity.

Mr Justice Cooke said:

'... it seems to me that in considering an appeal the Minister is entitled to ask himself whether the proposed development is compatible with the proper and desirable use of other land in the area.'

He therefore regarded the likelihood of interference with the telescope as both a planning consideration and a material consideration.

The fact that a policy protects particular occupiers is not, of itself, unlawful providing there is a proper planning purpose behind it. Furthermore, the 'human factor' can be taken into account in exceptional circumstances.

Great Portland Estates plc v Westminster City Council (1984)

Planning policies were formulated to preserve industrial activities which added to the vitality and functioning of Westminster but which were threatened by the pressure for more profitable office development. Great Portland Estates alleged that these policies were unlawful in that they were concerned with the protection of individual users rather than the development and use of land. The House of Lords held that these policies served a planning purpose. Inevitably this would mean that certain existing occupiers would be protected, but this was not the planning purpose. In reaching this decision Lord Scarman, who delivered the judgment of the House, said:

'Personal circumstances of an occupier, personal hardship, the difficulties of businesses which are of value to the character of a community are not to be ignored in the administration of planning control. It would be inhuman pedantry to exclude from the control of our development the human factor ... It can, however, and sometimes should, be given direct effect as an exceptional or special circumstance.'

The existing use

The preservation of the existing use may be a material consideration so long as that use is realistic.

Clyde & Co v Secretary of State for the Environment (1977)

Planning permission for a building permitted the western half to be used for offices and the eastern half for flats. After the building was erected the respondents sought planning permission to change the use of the flats to offices. Permission was refused, principally on the ground that such a change would result in the loss of residential accommodation of which there was a shortage.

The Court of Appeal held that the need for housing was a material consideration upon which the Secretary of State was entitled to base his decision.

The retention of a particular type of housing accommodation may be a material consideration.

Mitchell v Secretary of State for the Environment (1994)

Planning permission was sought to change the use of a house in multiple occupation as 20 bedsits to use as seven self-contained flats. Permission was refused by the Secretary of State on the ground that there was a need for multiple occupation for those who needed cheap housing. The Secretary of State's decision was upheld by the Court of Appeal. Material considerations were not confined to strict questions of amenity or environmental impact and the need for housing in a particular area was a material consideration. No sensible distinction could be drawn between a need for housing generally and a need for particular types of housing.

Affordable housing

In the *Mitchell* case, above, Lord Justice Balcombe supported the statement in Planning Policy Guidance Note 3 that a community's need for affordable housing is a material consideration. This matter came up for further consideration in *R v London Borough of Tower Hamlets, ex parte Barratt Homes*.

R v London Borough of Tower Hamlets, ex parte Barratt Homes (2000)

Tower Hamlets intended to take policies in the development plan into account in dealing with an application for a 'windfall' site for housing (a site not specified in the plan, but identified after adoption or approval of the plan). These policies sought the provision of one affordable housing unit for every three private housing units. Barratt claimed that a windfall site could not have an adverse effect on the need for affordable housing, so it would do no harm if no affordable housing was provided on the site.

Mr Justice Sullivan held that, as the evidence showed that allocated housing sites would not meet the identified need for affordable housing in the plan period, the release of this windfall site without making provision for affordable housing would have an adverse impact on the existing needs of the community for affordable housing. The shortfall would be even greater if an appropriate contribution were not sought from windfall sites.

'Precedent'

If the grant of permission on one site makes it difficult to refuse similar development on another site, this is a material consideration. There must be evidence for a reliance on the so-called precedent effect. In some cases the facts speak for themselves.

Collis Radio v Secretary of State for the Environment (1975)

Planning permission was refused for use of a warehouse as a retail warehouse. Although in itself the development would not be detrimental to existing shopping areas, if permission were granted it would lead to similar applications which would be difficult to refuse and the totality of permissions would be detrimental.

The appellant claimed that the prospect of proliferation of the same kind of use was not a proper consideration. In dismissing the appeal Lord Widgery CJ said:

> '... human nature being what it is, if permission is granted for a particular form of development on site A it is very difficult to refuse similar development on site B if the circumstances are the same. It must happen constantly in practice that a local planning authority refuses planning permission in respect of site A because of the consequences which it fears might flow in respect of sites B, C and D. No court has so far said that that is not a proper consideration to be adopted by a planning authority ...'

Poundstretcher, Harris Queensway v Secretary of State for the Environment and Liverpool City Council (1988)

In a case concerning the refusal of permission for two retail warehouses to sell certain goods, the appellants claimed that mere fear or a generalised concern of a precedent effect was not enough. The judge agreed, but was satisfied that there was evidence in this case. He said:

111

'There must be evidence in one form or another for the reliance on precedent. In some cases the facts may speak for themselves. For instance in the common case of the rear extension of one of a row or terrace of dwellings it may be obvious that other owners in the row are likely to want extensions if one is permitted. Another clear example is sporadic development in the countryside.'

It should be noted that commercial competition is not, of itself, a material consideration. However, this does not preclude a refusal of permission where the result of increased competition has a detrimental effect on the viability of an existing retail centre as in *Poundstretcher*.

Planning history and consistency of decisions

Previous planning decisions on the site in question are capable of being material considerations. Consistency is desirable; inconsistency may occur if an inspector or a planning authority fails to have regard to a previous decision. Reasons must be given for departing from previous decisions.

North Wiltshire District Council v Secretary of State for the Environment and Clover (1992)

An application for residential development was granted on appeal to the Secretary of State in 1990. The inspector made no reference in his decision to a refusal of permission by another inspector in 1982 in respect of a similar application. The Court of Appeal quashed the decision.

Lord Justice Mann said:

'It was not disputed in argument that a previous appeal decision is capable of being a material consideration. The proposition is in my judgment indisputable ... I do not suggest, and it would be wrong to do so, that like cases must be decided alike. An inspector must always exercise his own judgment. He is therefore free upon consideration to disagree with the judgment of another but before doing so he ought to have regard to the importance of consistency and to give his reasons for departure from the previous decision.'

As no such reasons were given, the decision was flawed.

Finance and enabling development

Cost and financial matters are capable of being material considerations.

Sosmo Trust v Secretary of State for the Environment and Camden London Borough Council (1983)

The only proposed scheme for development of a site that would produce an economic return involved a six-storey office development contrary to the local plan. The Secretary of State refused permission even though this would result in the site remaining derelict as the other schemes would not be implemented. He considered that the financial aspects of the development were irrelevant. In the High Court Mr Justice Woolf quashed this decision. He stated that cost can be a relevant consideration and pointed out that:

'what would be significant was not the financial viability or lack of financial viability of a particular project but the consequences of that financial viability or lack of financial viability.'

R v Westminster City Council, ex parte Monahan (1989)

Permission was granted for the extension and improvement of the Opera House at Covent Garden. The grant also permitted the erection of office accommodation on part of the site. Although this was a departure from the development plan it was necessary to fund the improvements to the Opera House. The Covent Garden Community Association challenged the grant of permission on the ground that the inclusion of office accommodation for financial reasons was not a material consideration.

The Court of Appeal dismissed the challenge. Lord Justice Kerr said:

'Financial constraints on the economic viability of a desirable planning development are unavoidable facts of life in an imperfect world. It would be unreal and contrary to common sense to insist that they must be excluded from the range of considerations which may properly be regarded as material in determining planning applications. Where they are shown to exist they may call for compromises or even sacrifices in what would otherwise be regarded as the optimum from the point of view of the public interest.'

As the offices were not ulterior or extraneous but part of a composite development, their provision fairly and reasonably related to the proposed development.

Planning gain

An offered planning obligation is material if it has some connection with the development which is not de minimis (Lord Keith in *Tesco Stores Ltd v Secretary of State for the Environment* (1995)). This subject is covered in more detail below at 3.5.4.

The consideration of alternative sites

A planning application must be considered on its merits and should not normally be refused merely because a different location would be preferable. In general, the consideration of alternative sites is relevant only in exceptional circumstances.

R (on the application of Jones) v North Warwickshire Borough Council (2001)

'Generally speaking and I lay down no fixed rule ... such [exceptional] circumstances will particularly arise where the proposed development, although desirable in itself, involves, on the site proposed, such conspicuous adverse effects that the possibility of an alternative site lacking such drawbacks necessarily itself becomes, in the mind of a reasonable local authority, a relevant planning consideration upon the application in question.' (Lord Justice Laws)

The exceptional circumstances are not limited to those identified by Lord Justice Laws. So in *Phillips v Hutchison 3G (UK) Ltd* it was held that consideration of alternative sites can be relevant where the development plan or policy guidance makes it relevant, as in the case of Planning Policy Guidance Note 8 on telecommunications ('PPG8').

Phillips v First Secretary of State and Havant Borough Council and Hutchison 3G (UK) Ltd (2003)

H submitted an application for prior approval for the siting and appearance of a phone mast. In the application H wrongly stated that the search area for a mast covering a 'cell' of 1.5 to 2 kilometres is only 100 to 200 metres in diameter. In fact it would extend to 400 or even 800 metres. Objectors could not identify an appropriate alternative site within a 200 metre diameter which was appropriate and only discovered that the search area was larger after an inspector had granted approval on appeal from the local planning authority. The claimant sought judicial review and in resisting this H argued that, as the inspector had found the proposed site entirely acceptable in planning terms, the existence of alternative sites was not a material consideration (citing Lord Justice Laws, see above).

Mr Justice Richards disagreed. He said:

'[PPG8] makes consideration of alternatives an integral part of the process of assessment of an application for approval of the siting of telecommunications structures.'

He went on to say that where there are two alternative sites, a decision maker could lawfully refuse approval for one of those sites if the location of a mast on that site would give rise to substantially greater public concerns than its location on the alternative site. (This is subject to the rights of a landowner of a site – see *St Leger-Davey v Secretary of State for the Environment* (2005).)

Where there are rival planning applications for one permission, a comparative assessment of their planning merits may be a material consideration.

R (on the application of Chelmsford Car & Commercial Ltd) v Chelmsford Borough Council (2005)

Local plan policy only permitted development outside the boundary of a village where a local need for affordable housing could be shown. Two applications were made for 12 affordable dwellings; only one of the two developments was required. The planning authority granted permission to the interested party, and refused the claimant's request to carry out a comparative assessment on the ground that the claimant's application was problematic in terms of affordability and deliverability.

Mr Justice Sullivan held that the authority had failed to take account of a material consideration and quashed the permission. The two competing sites were considered at the same meeting and each had to make out a case justifying an exception to the plan policy. Whatever might be said about the relevance of alternative sites in general, common sense suggested that a comparison of the two sites would be a material consideration.

Public fears

Mere public opposition is not a material consideration. However, genuine public fears, even if not objectively based, are material considerations which can amount (perhaps rarely) to a good reason to justify refusal. They are an aspect of the 'human factor' (see *Great Portland Estates plc v Westminster City Council*, above).

Newport Borough Council v Secretary of State for Wales (1998)

The local planning authority refused planning permission for a chemical waste treatment plant against a background of substantial public opposition. Although experts' and consultees' opinions provided no valid basis for health fears, one of the grounds for refusal was the local community's perception that the development would be contrary to the public interest generally and their interests in particular. The Secretary of State granted permission on appeal and awarded costs against the local planning authority on the basis that public concern without substantial supporting evidence does not warrant refusal of permission. The local planning authority challenged the award of costs.

The Court of Appeal held that the Secretary had made an error of law. Perceived fears, even if not soundly based upon scientific or logical fact, are relevant planning considerations as they may affect the amenity of an area. Therefore they can amount, perhaps rarely, to a good reason for refusal of planning permission. So in considering the award of costs, the Secretary of State should have determined whether or not, upon the facts of the case, the perceived fears were of such little weight as to render the refusal by the council unreasonable. So the matter was remitted for reconsideration.

Justifiable fears of crime and anti-social behaviour were held to be material considerations in the *West Midlands Probation Committee* case.

West Midlands Probation Committee v Secretary of State for the Environment, Transport and the Regions (1998)

Planning permission was refused, on appeal, for a two-storey extension to a bail and probation hostel. The inspector found that local residents' apprehensions about crime and anti-social behaviour had some justification given the evidence about robberies and other disturbing incidents committed by bailees. West Midlands Probation Committee challenged the decision, contending that apprehension and fear are not material planning considerations as they do not relate to the character or use of the land.

Lord Justice Pill, delivering the judgment of the Court said:

'Fear and concern felt by occupants of neighbouring land is as real in this case as in one involving polluting discharges and as relevant to their reasonable use of land. The pattern of behaviour was such as could properly be said to arise from the use of the land as a bail and probation hostel and did not arise merely because of the identity of the particular occupier or of particular residents.'

The weight to give the apprehension and fear was a matter of planning judgment.

Public fears and concerns may be material if they have land use consequences.

117

R v Broadland District Council, ex parte Dove (1998)

Planning permission was granted to change the use of a hotel to a hostel and group home with staff flats. Local residents claimed that the planning officer's report to committee wrongly concluded that public concern relating to the nature and character of potential residents was not a land use planning issue. They also claimed that concerns over the safety of children leading to increased car trips to and from the nearby primary school by parents were material planning considerations.

The council conceded that the increase in car trips was a material consideration and the Court of Appeal agreed. The Court of Appeal also held that the concerns of objectors about anti-social behaviour were capable of being material considerations. Nevertheless, the Court of Appeal dismissed the challenge. The council had, in fact, considered the concerns of the objectors. Furthermore it was impossible to conclude that there was a real possibility that the issue of car trips would have made any difference to the council's decision.

Public fears and phone masts

PPG8 on telecommunications recognises that health considerations and public concern can be material considerations. However it states that if a proposed phone mast meets the International Commission on Non-Ionizing Radiation Protection ('ICNIRP') guidelines for public exposure, it should not be necessary for a local planning authority to consider further the health aspects and concerns. PPG8 also states that it is the government's firm view that the planning system is not the place for determining health safeguards.

T-Mobile UK Ltd and others v First Secretary of State (2004)

Planning permission was refused for the installation and extension of telecommunications equipment at an existing site on grounds of amenity. The inspector dismissed the appeal on matters relating to health risks despite the fact that he acknowledged that the development complied with the ICNIRP guidelines. He was concerned about the beam of greatest intensity falling upon nearby schools, even though the Stewart Report (on non-ionising radiation) indicated there would be no risk to young children where emissions are within ICNIRP guidelines.

The Court of Appeal held that the inspector had misunderstood government policy and set aside his decision. Government policy was clear – where the ICNIRP guidelines were satisfied and schools and parents assured that they are met there is no need to look any further either to an actual or perceived health risk.

Human rights and proportionality

Certain articles of the *European Convention on Human Rights and Fundamental Freedoms* form part of the law of England and Wales by virtue of the *Human Rights Act* 1998. In the context of material considerations, rights under Article 8 and Article 1 of the First Protocol are relevant.

Article 8

(a) 'Everyone has the right to respect for his private and family life, his home and his correspondence.

(b) There shall be no interference by a public authority with the exercise of this right except such as is in accordance with the law and is necessary in a democratic society in the interests of national security, public safety or the economic well-being of the country, for the prevention of disorder or crime, for the protection of health or morals, or for the protection of the rights and freedoms of others.'

Article 1 of the First Protocol

'Every natural or legal person is entitled to the peaceful enjoyment of his possessions. No one shall be deprived of his possessions except in the public interest and subject to the conditions provided for by law and by the general principles of international law.

The preceding provisions shall not, however, in any way impair the right of a State to enforce such laws as it deems necessary to control the use of property in accordance with the general interest or to secure the payment of taxes or other contributions or penalties.'

Proportionality

Any interference with a Convention right must be proportionate to the intended objective. It must not be arbitrary or unfair.

Article 8 is an integral part of the approach to material considerations – *Lough v First Secretary of State* (2004).

Lough v First Secretary of State and Bankside Developments Ltd (2004)

Planning permission was granted, on appeal, for a 20-storey building. Local residents challenged that decision on the basis that their Article 8 and First Protocol, Article 1 rights had been infringed. Article 8 was said to be engaged by a departure from the development plan involving loss of privacy, overlooking, loss of a view, loss of light, interference with television reception and diminution in value of properties. It was also claimed that diminution in value of homes interferes with the peaceful enjoyment of them under the First Protocol, Article 1. Furthermore there was no reference to proportionality in the inspector's decision letter.

In delivering the leading judgment, Lord Justice Pill said:

> 'Article 8 should in my view normally be considered as an integral part of the decision maker's approach to material considerations and not, as happened in this case, in effect as a footnote.'

Nevertheless the Court upheld the decision because the inspector struck a balance which was entirely in accord with the requirements of Article 8. It was also clear from the findings of fact that, even if there were an infringement of Article 8 rights, it was justified under Article 8(2) once one took into account the need to protect the 'rights and freedoms of others'.

The absence of the word 'proportionality' did not render the decision unsatisfactory. The concept of proportionality is inherent in the approach to decision making in planning law. The inspector's balancing exercise was sufficient to meet any requirement of proportionality.

Lord Justice Pill did not accept that diminution in value is a separate and distinct breach of the Articles.

'I readily accept that a diminution in value may be a reflection of loss of amenity and may be taken into account as demonstrating such loss and its extent ... A loss of value in itself does not involve a loss of privacy or amenity and it does not affect the peaceful enjoyment of possessions. Diminution of value in itself is not a loss contemplated by the Articles in this context ...The weighing of interests should not be converted into an exercise in financial accounting to determine the loss to the respective landowners and the community.'

3.3 PRESUMPTION IN FAVOUR OF THE DEVELOPMENT PLAN

3.3.1 Planning and Compulsory Purchase Act 2004, section 38(6)

'If regard is to be had to the development plan* for the purpose of any determination to be made under the planning Acts the determination must be made in accordance with the plan unless material considerations indicate otherwise.'

* The new-style development plan under the *Planning and Compulsory Purchase Act* 2004 will be the regional spatial strategy (in Greater London, the spatial development strategy) together with the development plan documents for the relevant area. Conflicting policies within the development plan are to be resolved in favour of the last document adopted, approved or published. See section 38.

This provision replaces section 54A of the 1990 Act, but the wording is almost identical. The following case law relates to section 54A, but is of direct relevance in determining the meaning of its replacement.

Section 54A

'Where, in making any determination under the planning Acts, regard is to be had to the development plan, the determination shall be made in accordance with the plan unless material considerations indicate otherwise.'

'In accordance with the plan unless material considerations indicate otherwise'

The provision creates a presumption in favour of the plan. But all that is required to rebut the presumption is that 'material considerations indicate otherwise'. Strong contrary planning grounds are not required.

St Albans City and District Council v Secretary of State for the Environment and Allied Breweries (1993)

The planning authority challenged an inspector's decision on the ground that he had not applied section 54A. They contended that there must be strong contrary planning grounds to justify a departure from the development plan, and reference was made to the then current Planning Policy Guidance Note 1 which stated that an applicant 'would need to produce convincing reasons to demonstrate why the plan should not prevail'.

The judge preferred the words of the statute. He said:

'Undoubtedly section 54A does set up a presumption in favour of the development plan, but for its rebuttal it is sufficient if there are "material indications which indicate otherwise".'

The judge observed that a failure to refer expressly to section 54A is not fatal so long as the requirements are met.

Judicial interpretation of section 54A

The House of Lords gave guidance on the meaning of section 54A in *City of Edinburgh v Secretary of State for Scotland* (1998).

City of Edinburgh v Secretary of State for Scotland (1998)

Lord Clyde, delivering the judgment of the House, said:

'... if the application accords with the development plan and there are no material considerations indicating that it should be refused, permission should be granted. If the application does not accord with the development plan it will be refused unless there are material considerations indicating that it should be granted. One example of such a case may be where a particular policy in the plan can be seen to be outdated and superseded by more recent guidance. Thus the priority given to the development plan is not a mere mechanical preference for it. There remains a valuable element of flexibility. If there are material considerations indicating that it should not be followed then a decision contrary to its provisions can properly be given ...'

Lord Clyde also observed that the assessment of facts and the weighing of the considerations is still in the hands of the decision maker.

> 'As Glidewell LJ observed in *Loup v Secretary of State for the Environment* (1995) "What section 54A does not do is to tell the decision maker what weight to accord either to the development plan or to other material considerations". Those matters are left to the decision maker to determine in the light of the whole material before him both in the factual circumstances and in any guidance in policy which is relevant to the particular issues.'

Conflicting policies and the application of section 54A

In some cases it will be obvious that a proposal is or is not in accordance with the development plan. In others it may be more complex and so the decision maker should state whether or not he considers it to be in accordance with the plan in order to demonstrate that he has applied section 54A properly.

City of Edinburgh v Secretary of State for Scotland (1998)

Lord Clyde said:

> '[The decision maker] will also have to consider whether the development proposed in the application before him does or does not accord with the development plan. There may be some points in the plan which support the proposal but there may be some considerations pointing in the opposite direction. He will be required to assess all of these and then decide whether in light of the whole plan the proposal does or does not accord with it.'

R v Leominster District Council, ex parte Pothecary (1997)

Lord Justice Robert Walker said:

'This appeal shows that there are cases, of which this is a striking example, when the first stage must be for the decision maker to decide whether the proposed development is or is not in accordance with the development plan. Sometimes, of course, the answer to that question will be obvious ... But more often the development plan will (as in the City of Edinburgh Council case, and as in this case) contain exceptions, qualifications, overlapping or even contradictory policies and issues on which value judgments have to be made. In such cases it is desirable that planning officers should state their perception as to whether or not any proposed development is in accordance with the development plan, and that the planning authority should state whether or not they accept and agree with the officers' advice. I do not intend to give any encouragement to the lengthy recital of policies as a matter of rote. What is important is for it to be apparent how the decision maker has approached the important new statutory duty imposed by section 54A.'

Use of the word 'normally' in plan policies

Where a plan policy includes the word 'normally' (for example, 'development in the green belt will not normally be permitted') it has been contended that a proposal is still within the plan policy if it can be justified by other material considerations. Such an approach is wrong in law.

Sefton Metropolitan Borough Council v Secretary of State for Environment, Transport and the Regions (2002)

Mr Justice Ouseley said:

'If an Inspector interprets the word "normal" as meaning that a proposal can accord with a plan because of the effect of other material considerations, that, in my judgment, is an error of law. Such an approach would mean the rest of section 54A after "the development plan" would have no role. The words "other material considerations indicating otherwise" would all fall to be dealt with as part of the first stage in the decision making process, i.e. considering whether the proposal accorded with the development plan ...'

However, Mr Justice Ouseley recognised it might be different if specific exceptions are spelled out in the plan, and the proposal falls within one of them:

'It may be the case that if the content of the exceptional circumstances ... are spelled out, with specific planning aims attached to them, the satisfaction of those exceptional circumstances may mean that a proposal accords with the policy and the plan.'

3.4 PLANNING CONDITIONS

Section 70(1) of the 1990 Act provides that where an application is made to a local authority for planning permission, they may grant planning permission either unconditionally or subject to such conditions as they think fit.

As already seen in *City of London Corporation v Secretary of State for the Environment* (1971), a planning condition may restrict the operation of the *Use Classes Order*.

3.4.1 Specific conditions

Section 72 grants further specific powers to attach conditions, including conditions attaching to land under the control of the applicant (section 72(1)(a)). It also authorises conditions requiring the permitted buildings or works to be removed, a permitted use to be discontinued, and land to be reinstated, after a specified period (section 72(1)(b)).

Planning permission granted for a limited period – section 72(1)(b)

A temporary permission cannot be implied by the terms of the grant. For a planning permission to be granted for a limited period, a condition under section 72(1)(b) must be specifically imposed.

I'm Your Man Ltd v Secretary of State for the Environment, Transport and the Regions (1998)

On appeal, an inspector granted permission for the use of buildings for 'sales, exhibitions and leisure activities for a temporary period of seven years'. No condition was imposed requiring cessation of that use at the end of seven years.

In later proceedings, the appellant claimed that the permission was in effect permanent, as no condition had been attached. The Secretary of State claimed that the effect of the permission was to impose a 'limitation', and that breach of a limitation was subject to enforcement under section 171A of the 1990 Act.

The judge held that the 1990 Act does not provide for the imposition of limitations on the grant of permission pursuant to an application. The reference to limitations in the enforcement provision of the 1990 Act is a reference to limitations imposed under a development order. The failure to impose a condition became immune from challenge after six weeks (by virtue of section 284), so the permission became permanent in effect.

3.4.2 Limiting words

Where the grant of permission uses terms which restrict its scope, this may have an effect similar to the imposition of a condition. However, where the developer goes beyond the scope of such a permission, this is not a breach of condition as no condition has been imposed. So whether his activity is a breach of planning control depends on whether it is development or not.

Wilson v West Sussex County Council (1963)

Planning permission was granted for the erection of an 'agricultural cottage'.

The Court of Appeal held that the words 'agricultural cottage' mean a cottage whose use was limited to, or intended for, occupation by a person substantially engaged in agriculture. The permission therefore 'specified the purpose for which the building was used' under section 18(3) of the *Town and Country Planning Act* 1947 (now section 75(2)). The grant did not create any implied condition, but a change from agricultural occupation to a different form of occupation would be a change of use which could be material. Lord Justice Danckwerts went so far as to say it would, in his opinion, be a material change.

3.4.3 Validity of planning conditions – the Newbury tests

Although section 70(1) states that a local planning authority may impose such conditions as they think fit, this power can only be exercised for proper planning reasons. Conditions which are not for a planning purpose, or do not fairly and reasonably relate to the permitted development, or which are manifestly unreasonable, may be quashed by the courts.

Newbury District Council v Secretary of State for the Environment (1980)

The appellant sought planning permission to use existing hangars on an airfield for the storage of synthetic rubber. Permission was granted subject to a condition that the hangars be removed after ten years. The appellant contested the validity of the condition.

The House of Lords extracted three tests from the case law (now usually referred to as the 'Newbury tests') for determining the validity of planning conditions:

1   The condition must be for a planning purpose.

2   The condition must fairly and reasonably relate to the permitted development.

3   The condition must not be *Wednesbury* unreasonable, i.e. so unreasonable that no reasonable authority would ever impose it.

The House of Lords held that the condition failed test 2. The permission was merely for a change of use of existing substantial buildings.

(The House also determined that, in any event, no planning permission had been required, for the previous and the proposed use were both within Class X of the *Use Classes Order* 1950.)

The *Newbury* tests are a way of expressing the judicial principles which had been developed in the cases. Other ways of describing invalidity have been used in earlier decisions, including those of the House of Lords. The tests are neither exclusive nor exhaustive. But most cases can be usefully placed in one or more of the *Newbury* categories.

3.4.3.1 Must be for a planning purpose

Although some years before the House of Lords set out the three *Newbury* tests, the decision in *R v Hillingdon London Borough Council, ex parte Royco Homes* (1974) is now usually categorised as a case about conditions which were imposed for an ulterior purpose. Arguably the conditions concerned fail all three of the *Newbury* tests.

The case also confirmed that the remedy of *certiorari* (now called a quashing order) can be sought in the High Court to quash a determination of a local planning authority acting in excess of their legal authority.

R v Hillingdon London Borough Council, ex parte Royco Homes (1974)

Royco Homes owned land which the London Borough of Hillingdon wished to acquire for municipal housing. Royco sought permission for residential development and, eventually, permission was granted subject to certain conditions. One of the conditions required the first occupiers to be people on the housing waiting list of the council. Another required the houses to be occupied, in the first ten years, by tenants under the protection of the *Rent Act* 1977.

The Court of Appeal held that these conditions were ultra vires. They were unreasonable in the sense in *Hall & Co v Shoreham-by-Sea Urban District Council* (1964), below, as they required a private developer to take on at his own expense a part of the statutory duty of the housing authority.

It does not follow from the *Royco Homes* case that a developer cannot lawfully be required to provide a proportion of affordable housing where there is an identified need. See the *Barratt Homes* case, below. Furthermore, what cannot be achieved by a planning condition (such as funding of the provision by commuted payments) may be achievable by a planning obligation (see 3.5).

R v London Borough of Tower Hamlets ex parte Barratt Homes (2000)

In this case, examined above, Mr Justice Bridge made the following observations on the *Royco* decision.

'Royco was an extreme case ...'

'A perfectly proper planning requirement may be increased so as to become an unreasonable demand and an unlawful shifting of the burden ...'

'Most new social housing is now provided by registered social landlords (RSLs) ... The Council, so far as it is able, facilitates that process by ... grant aid to RSLs for new build schemes, *and by the exercise of its powers as local planning authority.*' [Author's emphasis]

3.4.3.2 Must fairly and reasonably relate to the permitted development

This rule was originally set out in the *Pyx Granite* case.

Pyx Granite Co Ltd v Ministry of Housing and Local Government (1958)

Lord Denning said:

'Although the planning authorities are given very wide powers to impose "such conditions as they think fit", nevertheless the law says that those conditions, to be valid, must fairly and reasonably relate to the permitted development. The planning authority are not at liberty to use their powers for an ulterior object, however desirable that object may seem to them to be in the public interest.'

So conditions governing the crushing and screening of stone on land near a quarry would be valid as they were in connection with the development.

Delta Design & Engineering Ltd v Secretary of State for the Environment, Transport and the Regions (2000)

Planning permission was granted for the change of use of Newton Hall, a listed building, to use for research and development. The permission was subject to a condition that part of a barn in the grounds be demolished in order to improve the approach to, and setting of, the Hall. The appellant challenged the condition on the ground that it was unrelated to the change of use of Newton Hall.

The Court of Appeal quashed the condition. The planning inspector's approach that the condition would improve the setting and appearance of the Hall was contrary to the approach in *Newbury*. Lord Justice Pill said:

> 'In my judgment there is great force in the appellant's submission that a change of use that involves no change in the appearance of the building, which it was the object of the listing to preserve, cannot be made conditional upon the demolition of an ancillary building in the grounds.'

3.4.3.3 Must not be Wednesbury unreasonable

The concept of Wednesbury or obvious unreasonableness comes from *Associated Provincial Picture Houses v Wednesbury Corporation* (1947).

Associated Provincial Picture Houses v Wednesbury Corporation (1947)

In this case Lord Green MR said:

> '... the court is entitled to investigate the action of the local authority with a view to seeing whether it has taken into account matters which it ought not to take into account, or, conversely, has refused to take into account or neglected to take into account matters which it ought to take into account. Once that question is answered in favour of the local authority, it may still be possible to say that the local authority, nevertheless, have come to a conclusion so unreasonable that no reasonable authority could ever have come to it. In such a case, again, I think the court can interfere ... the task of the court is not to decide what it

thinks reasonable, but to decide whether the condition imposed by the local authority is one which no reasonable authority, acting within the four corners of their jurisdiction, could have decided to impose ...'

A planning condition requiring the provision of what was virtually a public highway at private expense has been held to be so unreasonable as to be ultra vires and void.

Hall & Co v Shoreham-by-Sea Urban District Council (1964)

The plaintiffs applied for planning permission for a concrete plant on a site next to the congested Brighton road. To avoid further congestion and for traffic safety, conditions were attached requiring the plaintiffs to construct an ancillary road on their own land at their own expense. It was to run parallel to the main road, and give right of passage over it to and from such ancillary roads as may be constructed on adjoining land. The plaintiffs sought a declaration that the conditions were void.

The Court of Appeal held that, although the conditions were for good planning reasons related to the development, the conditions were so unreasonable as to be void under the principles in *Wednesbury*. The effect would be to convert a portion of the plaintiffs' land into a virtual public highway with no compensation and maintainable at their own expense.

The conditions could not be severed from the planning permission, so that was void also.

Bradford City Council v Secretary of State for the Environment and McLean Homes Northern Ltd (1986)

Planning permission was granted for housing development adjacent to a narrow road that was already overloaded. A condition required the road to be widened by one metre before the dwellings were occupied.

The Court of Appeal held that the condition was manifestly unreasonable. Little distinction could be made between the case and *Hall & Co v Shoreham* except that the authority contended that the developer had agreed to its terms. Even if this were the case, it would make no difference as vires cannot be conferred by consent.

Although settled law, *Hall & Co v Shoreham* has been criticised for preventing local authorities from requiring developers to make contributions to road improvements for the additional traffic burden they generate. However, planning law has evolved to enable this to be done by the use of *Grampian* conditions and planning obligations (see 3.4.3.4, below).

Conditions removing existing use rights

It is not unlawful for a planning condition to take away existing use rights without compensation. The adoption of the permission gives up the existing use rights.

Prossor v Minister of Housing and Local Government (1968)

Planning permission was granted for the rebuilding of a petrol service station on condition that no retail sales other than the sale of motor accessories should be carried out. After the permission was implemented, the appellant claimed that the sale of cars was an existing use right and that the condition could not remove it.

Lord Parker CJ said that by adopting the permission the appellant's predecessor had given up any existing use rights he may have had. The planning history of the site began afresh with the grant of a planning permission which was taken up and used. So the appellant was in breach of the planning condition.

Kingston-upon-Thames Royal London Borough Council v Secretary of State for the Environment (1974)

British Railways Board obtained planning permission to rebuild a station. Permission was granted subject to a condition that certain land to the south of the station and owned by the Board be used for car parking and no other purpose. This land had within it an electric traction cable, carried in a conduit, which supplied the electricity for the trains using the line. The Board challenged the validity of the condition.

The High Court held that the condition was valid in law. There is no rule of law that a condition cannot restrict existing uses without compensation. Mr Justice Bridge also observed that, as the 1990 Act specifically authorises the imposition of a condition to regulate the use of, or require works on, land other than the application site, it must encroach by its very nature on the applicant's rights over that land.

Conditions void for uncertainty

A condition will only be void for uncertainty if it cannot be given a sensible meaning. The court will strive to make sense of ambiguous terms.

Fawcett Properties v Buckingham County Council (1960)

In 1952 planning permission was granted for the erection of a pair of farm workers' cottages on condition that 'the occupation of the houses shall be limited to persons whose employment or latest employment is or was employment in agriculture as defined by [section] 119(1) of the *Town and Country Planning Act 1957*, or in forestry, or in an industry mainly dependent upon agriculture and including also the dependants of such persons as aforesaid'. The site was within an area designated as proposed green belt. The cottages were acquired by a property company who contended that the condition was void for uncertainty. It was argued, for example, that a Canadian fur trapper could fall within the definition.

The House of Lords held that the condition was valid. Lord Denning stated that a planning condition is only void for uncertainty if it can be given no sensible or ascertainable meaning, and not merely because it is ambiguous or leads to absurd results. So the agricultural restriction would be limited to persons who are employed in agriculture in the locality or in a local industry directly dependent on agriculture in the locality (such as a blacksmith).

M J Shanley (in liquidation) v Secretary of State for the Environment and South Bedfordshire District Council (1982)

A planning condition required local people to be given the first opportunity to buy houses within a development. Notwithstanding the high degree of uncertainty required to make the condition void according to the House of Lords in the *Fawcett* case, Mr Justice Woolf held that the condition was void. It did not give any indication at all as to the method or terms upon which the first opportunity was to be offered. It would be incapable, in practice, of being enforced.

Where a condition is unambiguous, no extraneous words are to be implied. See 2.4 on the interpretation of planning permission.

Sevenoaks District Council v First Secretary of State (2004)

Permission for a golf course was subject to a condition that, prior to the commencement of the development, details of associated engineering works should be submitted to, and approved in writing by, the local planning authority.

The condition failed to require that the works be carried out in accordance with the approval. Details were submitted and approved but the developer erected earth bunds higher than the approval specified. The authority served an enforcement notice alleging breach of condition, but the inspector allowed the developer's appeal with costs on the basis that the condition had been complied with. The authority appealed on the basis that compliance with the approved works was implied by the condition.

Mr Justice Sullivan held that as a planning permission is a public document it was essential that any obligation was clearly and expressly imposed. Where a condition is unambiguous, no extraneous words were to be implied.

Circular 11/95 gives guidance on the use and drafting of planning conditions and provides that a condition should be necessary, relevant to planning, relevant to the development, enforceable, precise and reasonable. A condition which does not meet the requirements of clarity and precision in Circular 11/95, and which is unreasonable in the ordinary sense of the word, is not necessarily manifestly unreasonable in the *Newbury* sense.

Dilieto v Ealing London Borough Council (1998)

A planning condition required a yard to be 'maintained clear at all times to the satisfaction of the local planning authority'.

The Divisional Court held that, although the words 'to the satisfaction of the local planning authority' introduced a degree of uncertainty and the condition was unlikely to meet the requirements of the Circular, it was not void. The basic obligation was to keep the yard clear at all times and the additional words had the effect of allowing a degree of latitude.

Conditions on land outside the applicant's control

It has been seen that section 72(1)(a) specifically authorises the imposition of conditions for regulating the development or use of any land under the control of the applicant, whether or not it is land within the application. It also authorises the carrying out of works on any such land.

Section 72 is without prejudice to the general power to impose conditions in section 70. So a condition relating to land outside the application site and not within the control of the applicant is lawful if the applicant is able to comply with it (and it meets the *Newbury* criteria).

Davenport v Hammersmith and Fulham London Borough Council (1999)

D was granted planning permission in connection with the use of land for motor vehicle repairs, subject to a condition that 'no vehicles which have been left with or are in the control of the applicant shall be stored or parked in Tasso road'. D claimed that the condition was ultra vires section 72(1) as it related to land outside the application site and outside his control. He claimed that section 70 only related to on-site conditions.

The Divisional Court held that the condition was within the powers in section 70 and was valid. The condition was negative in effect and was plainly within the power of the applicant. All it required was that he did not use certain land outside his control for a stated purpose. No control of the land was needed in order to comply with the condition.

Where a condition requires control of the land it does not necessarily involve having an estate or interest in that land. It is a question of fact and degree.

George Wimpey & Co Ltd v New Forest District Council (1979)

The existing access to a development site was by housing estate roads. Such access was unsuitable for construction vehicles. So the applicants (Wimpey) entered into agreements with the adjoining owner under which they were granted a licence for a right of way for vehicles along a strip of land. However, the licence was terminable at any time by one month's notice if the use of the right of way interfered with the development of the adjoining land. So the Secretary of State refused planning permission on the basis that the agreements were not such that the land could be considered to be 'under the control of the applicant'.

The High Court stated that control does not necessarily involve having an estate or interest in land. It is therefore a question of fact and degree for the Secretary of State whether the control is of a degree and kind sufficient to satisfy him that the condition will be complied with. The control should be 'such as appears expedient for the purpose of implementing the condition'. So there was ample evidence for the Secretary of State to have come to the conclusion that there was insufficient control to impose a condition ensuring the construction traffic used the adjoining land.

(It was agreed that a condition prohibiting the use of estate roads for construction traffic would have been valid.)

A condition requiring something to be done outside the power of the applicant is unenforceable. Such a condition is *Wednesbury* unreasonable.

Mouchell Superannuation Fund Trustees v Oxfordshire County Council (1992)

A condition attached to a quarrying permission required access to the site to be by way of a particular road (a public highway) which was to be improved to the reasonable satisfaction of the County Surveyor.

The Court of Appeal held that the condition was unlawful. The applicant could not secure that all vehicles used the route prescribed. More fundamentally, the applicant could not carry out the necessary highway works of widening and improvement. The road and the adjacent land were outside his control. The works could only take place if the County Council exercised its powers under the *Highways Act* 1980.

3.4.3.4 Negative or 'Grampian' conditions

The solution to the *Mouchell* problem is to draft the condition negatively as was proposed in the *Grampian* case below. Instead of requiring the applicant to carry out the necessary works, the condition is worded so that the development or use of the application site cannot commence until the works have been carried out. Such a condition is enforceable – the development is unauthorised until such time as the condition is satisfied.

Grampian Regional Council v City of Aberdeen District Council (1984)

Grampian Regional Council applied for planning permission to change a large site from agricultural to industrial use. The matter was referred to a reporter on appeal. The reporter found that access to the site could be obtained via a road which led to a T-junction with a dual carriageway. This would create a traffic hazard justifying refusal. He considered that a condition requiring the closure of part of this road, thus forcing traffic to use a safer junction, could not be imposed as it would require the Secretary of State's confirmation of the closure. So the reporter refused permission. Grampian contended that the reporter could have attached a condition that the development was not to proceed unless and until the road was closed. The House of Lords agreed. Lord Keith said:

> 'There is a crucial difference between the positive and negative type of condition in this context. Namely that the latter is enforceable while the former is not.'

He stated that a negative condition still has to pass the *Wednesbury* test of reasonableness, but in this case it was 'not only not unreasonable but highly appropriate'. Lord Keith also observed that the fact that development might not take place is a natural feature of the planning process. There is nothing to compel any successful applicant for planning permission to carry out his development.

There is no rule of law that a *Grampian* condition is void unless it has a reasonable prospect of fulfilment. The question whether a condition, *Grampian* or otherwise, is unreasonable depends on the circumstances.

British Railways Board v Secretary of State for the Environment (1993)

British Rail applied for planning permission for housing. On appeal, the inspector recommended the provision of an access road by way of a *Grampian* condition. This would require Hounslow Council to enter into a section 52 agreement with British Rail. Hounslow refused to enter into such an agreement. So the Secretary of State refused permission on the basis that a *Grampian* condition would be void as there was no reasonable prospect of the access road being built. British Rail challenged this decision.

The House of Lords held that there is no absolute rule that the existence of difficulties, even if apparently insuperable, must necessarily lead to refusal of planning permission for a desirable development. Lord Keith observed that the 1990 Act provides that planning permission can be sought by a person who does not own the land the subject of the application and it would not be legitimate for a planning authority to refuse permission simply because the owner is opposed to development. The case was remitted to the Secretary of State.

3.4.4 Effect of striking out a void condition

In both the *Royco Homes* and *Hall & Co* cases, above, the effect of striking out a void condition was to render the whole planning permission void. This was because the conditions in those cases were fundamental to the permission. The House of Lords considered this issue in *Kent County Council v Kingsway Investments (Kent) Ltd* (1970).

Kent County Council v Kingsway Investments (Kent) Ltd (1970)

Two law lords were of the opinion that there might be cases where unimportant conditions could be severed (the prevailing view in the Court of Appeal decisions) but a third thought that the permission would always fail where a condition was struck out for invalidity. In this particular case, the condition was important so, if it had been void, the permission would have fallen.

3.4.5 Section 73 – application to modify conditions

Section 73 provides that an application may be made for planning permission without complying with conditions subject to which a previous planning permission was granted. The application cannot be made where development has not commenced within the time limit for commencement – section 73(4).

Pye v Secretary of State for the Environment, Transport and the Regions and North Cornwall District Council (1998)

Mr Justice Sullivan held that when considering an application under section 73, the local planning authority have to have regard to the factual circumstances as they exist at the time of their decision. If policies have changed, that must be taken into account. (This decision was approved by the Court of Appeal in *Powergen UK plc v Leicester City Council* (2000).)

He also observed that a section 73 application 'leaves the original permission intact and unamended'. (Compare this with an appeal under section 78 which carries the risk of the permission being refused altogether.)

Abolition of extension of time limits – section 73(5)

The *Planning and Compulsory Purchase Act* 2004 inserts section 73(5). This prohibits an application under section 73 to extend the time, or have the effect of extending the time, within which development must be started or an application made for approval of reserved matters.

3.5 PLANNING OBLIGATIONS – SECTION 106

It is appropriate to consider planning obligations here as they are usually connected to the grant of planning permission. They resemble planning conditions in some respects and are frequently put in place to achieve planning objects that cannot be achieved by way of conditions.

Under the *Planning and Compulsory Purchase Act* 2004 planning obligations are to be replaced by 'planning contributions' – charges for certain development set out in the development plan. However, the case law relating to obligations may still be of relevance because the power to negotiate an obligation instead of, or possibly as well as, a contribution may be preserved. There may also be development for which a planning contribution is not levied but for which an obligation could be appropriate.

3.5.1 Section 106

'Any person interested in land in the area of a local planning authority may, by agreement or otherwise, enter into an obligation ... :

(a) restricting the development or use of the land in any specified way;

(b) requiring specified operations or activities to be carried out in, on, under or over the land;

(c) requiring the land to be used in any specified way; or

(d) requiring a sum or sums to be paid to the authority on a specified date or dates or periodically.'

3.5.2 Use of section 106 obligations

Government policy is to restrict the use of obligations to those necessary to make the development acceptable in planning terms (Circular 05/05) and not as a form of development tax or betterment levy. But it is not easy to determine exactly what public infrastructure or external costs are appropriate for a developer to bear. Furthermore the test of necessity in the policy guidance is not the same as the legal test of validity (see the *Plymouth* and *Tesco Stores* cases, below). Consequently, developer contributions have been provided for a wide variety of community benefits beyond that required to overcome legitimate planning objections to the development. This has led to claims that permission is being bought and sold.

3.5.3 Validity of planning obligations

Planning obligations may validly incorporate terms which would be invalid if incorporated within a planning condition. Furthermore, a planning obligation is not invalid merely because it is contrary to the Secretary of State's planning policy.

Good v Epping Forest District Council (1993)

Planning permission had been granted for the erection of a house on a farm for a pig man. It was subject to the usual agricultural occupancy condition. This was reinforced by a section 52 agreement (section 52 of the *Town and Country Planning Act* 1971, the predecessor to section 106 of the 1990 Act) which reiterated the condition but also provided that the house should not be sold away or otherwise alienated from the remainder of the application site. A subsequent purchaser, wishing to sell the house off for non-agricultural occupancy, sought a declaration that the agreement was void in law because it sought to do what could not have been imposed by a condition as it would have been struck down by the Secretary of State on appeal. The Court of Appeal held that the agreement was valid. The fact that the Secretary of State might set aside the requirements in a planning condition is a material fact, but does not render unlawful the decision to make the requirements or the making of the agreement.

The Court also considered whether a requirement which could not be validly incorporated in a planning condition could be incorporated in a section 52 agreement. This turns on the application of the *Newbury* criteria to planning obligations. It was accepted that criterion 1 (must be for a planning purpose) and criterion 3 (must not be *Wednesbury* unreasonable) must apply. However, it was held that criterion 2 (it must fairly and reasonably relate to the permitted development) was not applicable. The powers under section 52 are distinct from those governing conditions.

> 'There would be little point in enacting section 52 ... if section 52 agreements were confined to those matters which could be dealt with by condition.' (Lord Justice Ralph Gibson)

Tesco Stores Ltd v Secretary of State for the Environment and West Oxfordshire District Council (1995)

'Of course it is normal for a planning obligation to be undertaken or offered in connection with an application for planning permission and to be expressed as conditional upon the grant of that permission. But once the condition has been satisfied, the planning obligation becomes binding and cannot be challenged by the developer or his successor in title on the ground that it lacked a sufficient nexus with the proposed development.' (Lord Hoffman)

Pye (J A) (Oxford) Ltd v South Gloucestershire District Council (2001)

Pye had entered into a section 52 agreement with the highway authority to fund a link road to overcome highway objections to its application for planning permission. In order to build the road, part of a disused railway would have to be purchased and Pye undertook to repay the highway authority the purchase price. When it transpired in Lands Tribunal proceedings that the land would cost £428,000, Pye claimed that the section 52 agreement was void on the basis that the link road had no connection with the development permitted on Pye's land.

The Court of Appeal held that if there were no connection, the planning permission would be void as it would be based on an immaterial consideration.

'But it does not follow that the agreement is in any way infected.' (Lord Justice Latham)

The agreement was within the terms of section 52 (for regulating the development or use of land) and there was nothing to suggest that the highway authority took account of anything other than proper highway or planning considerations when they entered it.

3.5.4 Validity of a connected planning permission

It has been shown that a planning obligation may be perfectly lawful even though it does not fairly and reasonably relate to the permitted development, so long as it satisfies *Newbury* criteria 1 and 3 and is intra vires section 106. However, the connected planning permission will be void if the decision maker, in determining whether to grant permission or not, took into account an unrelated planning obligation, for such an obligation is an immaterial consideration. If it is related, the weight to give it is a matter for the decision maker.

Tesco Stores Ltd v Secretary of State for the Environment and West Oxfordshire District Council (1995)

Tesco offered to fully fund the building of a new road to relieve severe traffic congestion, at a cost of £6.6m, if they were granted permission for a retail superstore. (There was no point in offering partial funding, for the road would not get built.) The Secretary of State refused permission. Tesco appealed on the basis that he had ignored a material consideration, namely their offer of funding.

The House of Lords held that the Secretary of State had not ignored the offer to fund the road but, because of the tenuous link with the superstore, had given it little weight.

'An offered planning obligation which has nothing to do with the proposed development, apart from the fact that it is offered by the developer, will plainly not be a material consideration and could be regarded only as an attempt to buy planning permission. If it has some connection with the proposed development which is not de minimis, then regard must be had to it. But the extent, if any, to which it should affect the decision is a matter entirely within the discretion of the decision-maker and in exercising that discretion he is entitled to have regard to his established policy.'

The Secretary of State had taken the view that, in accordance with his policy in Circular 16/91 on the acceptance of planning obligations, it was unreasonable to seek even a partial contribution in the circumstances of the case.

Tesco Stores sets a low threshold of materiality. Although weight is a matter for the decision maker, the grant of permission may be *Wednesbury* unreasonable where the obligation 'just crept across the threshold' of materiality and it was given the weight that no reasonable decision maker would give it.

R v South Holland District Council, ex parte Lincoln Co-operative Society Ltd (2000)

In 1998 planning permission was sought for a supermarket about 300 metres from the centre of a small country town. Permission was refused, largely because of the detrimental effect the development would have on the existing town centre. A second application was made in 1999 accompanied by an offer to pay £100,000 by way of a planning obligation. Against officer advice, the committee granted permission stating that the additional benefits provided by the £100,000 would 'outweigh' the adverse effect on the town.

Lady Justice Smith held that, although the obligation just 'crept across the threshold of materiality' the decision to grant permission was *Wednesbury* unreasonable. There had been no evaluation of what could be achieved with the £100,000 and the committee had no information upon which to act. The benefits which might be derived from the money were a matter of pure speculation. There were no rational grounds for believing that the obligation could significantly address the harm envisaged by the development, let alone outweigh it.

3.5.4.1 Policy and law

Government policy requires planning obligations to be used only where they are relevant to planning, necessary to make the development acceptable in planning terms, directly related to the development, fairly and reasonably related to the development in scale and in kind, and reasonable in all other respects.

However, according to the Court of Appeal in the *Plymouth* case (below) this is not a test of legal validity; the law (section 70(2) above) requires all material considerations to be taken into account, and is not limited to matters which a planning authority considers necessary.

R v Plymouth City Council, ex parte Plymouth and South Devon Co-operative Society Ltd (1993)

The draft local plan provided for a large food store at Marsh Mills. The plan said that the store was expected to provide 'substantial community benefits'.

Tesco and Sainsbury submitted applications for stores on two sites at Marsh Mills, so each company was invited to make submissions to the planning committee as to why its application should be preferred to the other. Both companies made offers of community benefits. Sainsbury's offer included the construction of a tourist information centre on the site, an art gallery display facility, a work of art in the car park, and a bird-watching hide overlooking the River Plym. It also offered to contribute £800,000 to the establishment of a park-and-ride facility in the neighbourhood and up to £1m for works to make another site suitable for industrial use (to replace the loss of the Sainsbury site).

The planning committee decided to grant both applications. South Devon Co-op contended that an offer of community benefits must be necessary in that it overcomes what would otherwise have been a planning objection to the development. Therefore the offers were immaterial considerations vitiating the grants of permission.

The Court of Appeal held that there is no additional legal test of necessity. Considerations are material if they are planning considerations and fairly and reasonably relate to the development. They must also pass the *Wednesbury* test. The offered benefits met these criteria. The fact that such matters might be given less weight on appeal does not mean that a planning authority is not entitled to treat them as material considerations.

The *Plymouth* decision was controversial. It was claimed by some academics that the judicial approach permitted something very close to the purchase and sale of planning permission. The decision was also expressly doubted by another member of the Court of Appeal (Lord Justice Steyn in his judgment in *Tesco Stores*).

The question of the buying and selling of permission was eventually considered by the House of Lords in the *Tesco Stores* case.

Tesco Stores Ltd v Secretary of State for the Environment and West Oxfordshire District Council (1995)

The judgment of the House was delivered by Lord Keith. He stated that it is 'axiomatic that planning consent cannot be bought and sold' but he did not dissent from the decision in *Plymouth* the effect of which, he said, is:

'simply that a local planning authority is not acting unlawfully if it fails to apply a necessity test in considering whether a planning obligation should be required.'

But he also commented that there was nothing unlawful about the Secretary of State's policy on necessity. He observed that the references in the Circular to planning obligations being necessary:

'mean no more than that a planning obligation should not be given weight unless the exercise of planning judgment indicates that permission ought not to be granted without it, not that it is to be completely disregarded as immaterial.'

Looking at the decision letter as a whole, the Secretary of State had not ignored Tesco's offer to fund a new road, but given it little weight as he was entitled to do.

3.5.5 Refusal of permission unless obligation entered into

The application of the *Wednesbury* test to planning conditions produces different results when applied in the context of planning obligations. Whereas it would be *Wednesbury* unreasonable to impose a condition requiring, for example, the payment of money towards road improvements, it would be perfectly legitimate to refuse permission unless the developer is willing to undertake a planning obligation to fund improvements necessitated by the development. There is no statutory requirement that all the related infrastructure must be provided by public money.

'... the test of Wednesbury unreasonableness applied in Hall & Co v Shoreham is quite inconsistent with the modern practice in relation to planning obligations which has been encouraged by the Secretary of State ... and Parliament in the new [section] 106 ...' (Lord Hoffman, *Tesco Stores Ltd v Secretary of State* (1995))

R v South Northamptonshire District Council, ex parte Crest Homes plc (1994)

A proposed alteration to the Northamptonshire structure plan would mean that Towcester would have to accommodate so much new residential development that it would nearly double in population. Accordingly the council explored with a group of the main developers, including Crest Homes, what infrastructure was needed, its cost, the extent of the contribution the developers were prepared to make and how that contribution would be made. It was agreed that each developer should make a financial contribution which was a percentage of the enhancement in land value attributable to the grant of permission and that the whole fund would go to the provision of essential infrastructure and services. This would be embodied in section 106 agreements.

Crest withdrew from the group and did not enter a section 106 agreement. Their subsequent application for planning permission was refused and the refusal was upheld on appeal. Crest then challenged the legality of the whole process contending that the council was selling planning permission.

The Court of Appeal held that the council had acted lawfully. It was perfectly legitimate to require a financial contribution to cover the costs of infrastructure related to the development. Such a requirement is for a planning purpose, fairly and reasonably relates to the development and is not *Wednesbury* unreasonable. Furthermore the percentage formula was a legitimate method to pay for the costs. On the facts, it was a genuine pre-estimate of the developer's proper contribution and there was no suggestion that it would raise a disproportionate amount.

3.5.6 Scope of section 106 obligations

An obligation for the provision of off-site works that does not fall within the categories set out in section 106(1) can be achieved by the use of a negative condition in the obligation (akin to a *Grampian* condition).

R v Canterbury City Council, ex parte Springimage Ltd (1993)

The council resolved to enter into a section 106 agreement which would include a provision restricting the developer's freedom to connect to the present, inadequate, sewage system. (So sewerage works would have to be undertaken.) It was contended that section 106 does not provide for agreements about requisitioning sewers.

The judge held that the desired result could be achieved by a negative provision in the agreement restricting the development of the application site until proper sewerage arrangements had been made.

Land transfer

An obligation to transfer land does not, of itself, fall within section 106. However, it can be brought within section 106 if it includes provisions 'restricting the development or use of land in any specified way' under section 106(1)(a), or 'requiring the land to be used in any specified way' under section 106(1)(c) – *R v South Northamptonshire District Council, ex parte Crest Homes plc* (1994). A transfer of land cannot be imposed upon an authority by way of a unilateral undertaking for it does not directly restrict development or use of land nor fall within the other powers set out in section 106(1) (such as the payment of money).

Wimpey Homes Holdings v Secretary of State for the Environment and Winchester City Council (1993)

Wimpey sought planning permission for development which would necessitate the provision of open space. Wimpey executed a deed containing unilateral undertakings to transfer the open space to the city council and to pay a lump sum for its maintenance, subject to the grant of permission. The council considered the lump sum to be inadequate and permission was refused. One of the issues in subsequent proceedings in the High Court was whether the unilateral undertaking was a valid obligation under section 106. It was held that it was not. Without covenants on the part of the council it did not impose a restriction on development or use. Nevertheless, it was a material consideration to be taken into account in determining the application. The judge suggested that Wimpey could put forward a deed imposing restrictions on land to secure the provision of open space and either retain that land or transfer it to a trustee.

Payment of money

Section 106(1)(d) includes the payment of money to the local planning authority. The payment of money to another is therefore outside paragraph (d) but it may fall within paragraph (b) if it is to be used for specified operations or activities to be carried out on land.

South Oxfordshire District Council v Secretary of State for the Environment (1994)

The trustees of the Mapledurham estate sought planning permission for a 36-hole golf course. The purpose was to fund the repair (at a cost of £1.7m) of a number of listed buildings on the estate. One of the issues was whether a unilateral undertaking for that purpose was a nullity as not falling within the categories in section 106(1). The relevant provision was 'to use all reasonable endeavours to dispose of the site by way of a long building lease or otherwise and thereafter within a period of 20 years to utilise all relevant income' for repairs to the listed buildings and curtilages.

It was held that, although this provision did not fall within paragraph (d) it fell within paragraph (b) as it required specified operations or activities to be carried out.

Money deposited with the authority for infrastructure works is held in 'a form of trust'

Where funds are provided to an authority for specified purposes under the terms of a planning obligation, this creates a form of trust. Thus the authority can be held to account.

Patel v Brent London Borough Council (2005)

The appellants deposited £550,000 with the local authority for highway improvements. Any unexpended balance was to be returned to the appellants. The section 106 agreement required the authority to use their reasonable endeavours to complete the improvements within two years of the grant of planning permission. In fact it took ten years. It was contended that the agreement was discharged by repudiatory breach and that the money should be refunded.

The Court of Appeal held that the terms of section 106A (under which an obligation can be modified or discharged by the local planning authority or the Secretary of State on appeal) precluded discharge under contract law. Nevertheless a form of trust had been created and some of the money had been spent on altering a junction on a tributary road not covered by the agreement. The council's claim that they could draw down funds for any works 'connected in some way' to the highway improvements required went too far. So there should be an inquiry into the extent of the work that satisfied the requirements of the planning obligation.

4

Enforcement

Enforcement cases that pre-date the reforms introduced by the *Planning and Compensation Act* 1991 should be used with care.

'I would suggest considerable caution before applying statements from pre-1991 cases to the new statutory regime, one of the purposes of which was to give a clear signal to the courts and others that the more legalistic features of current case-law and practice can be abandoned.' (Lord Justice Carnwath in *Fidler v First Secretary of State* (2004))

4.1 BREACH OF PLANNING CONTROL – SECTION 171A

Part VII of the 1990 Act contains the enforcement provisions.

Section 171A(1) provides that:

(a) 'carrying out development without the required planning permission, or

(b) failing to comply with any condition or limitation subject to which planning permission has been granted,

constitutes a breach of planning control.'

The planning authority cannot take enforcement action for breach of condition where the development does not comply in a material respect with the planning permission. In such a case the development is unauthorised so the condition cannot attach to it. Action should be taken under section 171A(1)(a).

Handoll v Warner Goodman Streat (1995)

Planning permission was granted for the erection of a building, subject to an agricultural occupancy condition. The building was erected some 90 feet west of the approved location. It was held that where development is carried out in breach of planning control, and not by way of implementation of any planning permission, the development is not subject to any conditions as it is unauthorised.

4.2 TIME LIMITS FOR ENFORCEMENT ACTION – SECTION 171B

4.2.1 Operational development

Section 171B sets out the time limits within which enforcement action must be taken. Where the breach consists of operational development, no enforcement action can be taken after the end of the period of four years beginning with the date on which the operations were substantially completed – section 171B(1).

The meaning of substantially completed was considered by the House of Lords in *Sage v Secretary of State*.

Sage v Secretary of State for the Environment, Transport and the Regions and Maidstone Borough Council (2003)

S erected an unfinished dwellinghouse. The ground floor was rubble and there were no service fittings, no staircase, no plaster and no glazing. S claimed that nothing that remained to be done was within the definition of development, as any remaining building operations were either internal or did not materially affect the external appearance. Therefore the building was substantially completed.

The House of Lords rejected this reasoning and adopted a 'holistic' approach. Regard must be had to the totality of the operations that were originally contemplated. This is in accordance with the principle that when detailed permission is granted then, unless the building is erected both externally and internally fully in accordance with the permission, the whole operation is unlawful. So if the builder has stopped short of what he intended to build, the building is uncompleted and the four-year period has not begun.

Operations completed more than four years previously are not immune if they are integral to an unlawful material change of use, as enforcement powers include that of requiring the land to be restored to its previous condition. (The ten-year rule applies to material changes of use.)

Murfitt v Secretary of State for the Environment and East Cambridgeshire District Council (1980)

The owner of a farmyard was using it for a haulage business. He extended the area of the farmyard for parking vehicles by laying down a quantity of hardcore. More than four years later, the planning authority served an enforcement notice alleging a material change of use of land to use for the parking of heavy goods vehicles and requiring the land to be restored by the removal of the hardcore. The appellant claimed that the hardcore could not be required to be removed as it was operational development immune from enforcement action.

It was held that the enforcement notice could require the removal of the hardcore as it was part and parcel of the use of the land for parking HGVs. Lord Justice Waller also observed that where the land is left useless, as in this case, it is logical to restore it to the condition in which it was before the unlawful use started.

It follows that operations which are integral to an unauthorised material change of use can be the subject of enforcement action, even though such operations are not development.

Somak Travel v Secretary of State for the Environment and Brent London Borough Council (1988)

The appellant operated a travel agency on the ground floor of a building. The first and second floors were used for residential accommodation. The appellant converted these floors into office space and installed a spiral staircase to connect the ground floor with the first floor. The local planning authority served an enforcement notice alleging a material change of use and requiring the spiral staircase to be removed. If the staircase were not removed, the first floor would be unlettable as it would be open to the ground floor with no privacy or security.

The appellant claimed that, as the erection of a spiral staircase did not require planning permission (being internal works) an enforcement notice could not lawfully require its removal.

The court held that it was lawful to require its removal. It was integral to, or part and parcel of, the change from residential to office use.

4.2.2   Change of use to a single dwellinghouse

In the case of a change of use of a building to use as a single dwellinghouse, section 171B(2) grants immunity from enforcement action upon the expiry of four years from the breach.

Does this immunity apply to the subdivision of a dwellinghouse into two or more separate dwellings? The Court of Appeal in the *Van Dyck* case said 'yes'.

Van Dyck v Secretary of State for the Environment; Doncaster Metropolitan Borough Council v Secretary of State for the Environment and Dunnill (1993)

These cases concerned the conversion of a dwellinghouse into separate flats.

Section 55(3)(a) states that use of a dwellinghouse as two separate dwellinghouses is a material change of use of the building and of each part. Building is defined in section 336 as including any part of a building. Therefore in the case of each new flat there is a change of use of part of the building to use as a single dwellinghouse. So the four-year rule applies.

It is obviously vital to identify the breach correctly in order to determine which time limits apply.

Moore v Secretary of State for the Environment, Transport and the Regions (1998)

The outbuildings of a large Edwardian country house were converted, without planning permission, into ten self-contained units of residential accommodation for the purpose of holiday lettings. One of the issues in the enforcement appeal was whether this was a material change of use to ten units of holiday accommodation, in which case the ten-year rule applied, or whether it was a change to ten single dwellinghouses, in which case the four-year rule applied. The Court of Appeal held that there was a change to ten single dwellinghouses as there was no requirement that a house must be occupied permanently in order to be a dwellinghouse (applying the *Gravesham* case, at 1.7.9.1).

R (on the application of Lee) v First Secretary of State and Swale Borough Council (2003)

A barn contained two caravans. Facilities within the barn together with the two caravans provided residential accommodation. The issue was whether or not there had been a change of use of a building to use as a single dwellinghouse, in which case the four-year rule applied. The inspector took the view that as the caravans were not part of the building, their use was not part of the use of the building. Without the caravans, there were insufficient facilities for day-to-day domestic living in the rest of the barn. So the four-year rule was not applicable.

The court held that the inspector had erred. It does not follow from the fact that the caravans are not part of the building that their use is not part of the use of the building. Where their use is residential in conjunction with the use of the building, it constitutes part of the use of the building. So the case was remitted for further consideration.

4.2.3 Any other breach

Under section 171B(3) there is immunity for any other breach after the end of a period of ten years beginning with the date of that breach. This covers any material change of use (except change to a single dwellinghouse) as well as breach of a condition or limitation.

Where a dwellinghouse is limited to seasonal or holiday occupation by condition, permanent occupation is a breach of that condition, not a material change of use to a single dwellinghouse. Therefore the ten-year rule applies.

Bloomfield v Secretary of State for the Environment, Transport and the Regions (1999)

Permission had been granted for the retention of a chalet subject to a condition that it be used for recreational purposes from April to October and not for permanent residential occupation. The storage of domestic and household effects was permitted from November to March. More than four years after the building had been used for permanent residential occupation, the local planning authority served an enforcement notice requiring such occupation to cease. The appellant claimed that as there had been a change of use from recreational and storage use to use as a single dwellinghouse, the four-year rule applied and the use was immune. The High Court held that the chalet was at all times a dwellinghouse, so there had been a breach of condition, not a material change of use. The recreational and storage uses are ordinarily incidental to the residential use.

4.2.4 Operation of ten-year rule

Immunity only arises if enforcement action could have been taken at any time during the ten-year period.

Thurrock Borough Council v Secretary of State for the Environment, Transport and the Regions (2002)

An enforcement notice was served in 1999 in respect of the use of land as an airfield. An inspector quashed the notice on the ground that the airfield use had begun more than ten years ago and had not been abandoned.

The Court of Appeal held that the inspector had erred. It is not sufficient that the use commenced more than ten years ago. The landowner must demonstrate, on the balance of probabilities, that it has continued throughout the ten years and so enforcement action could have been taken at any time. The concept of abandonment is applicable to established use rights and could only become relevant under the new rule once immunity has been established after ten years of continuing breach (when a lawful development certificate can be sought).

The Court accepted that an enforcement notice can lawfully be issued if the unlawful activity has temporarily ceased 'because it is the weekend or the factory's summer holiday, for instance'. But once the activity has permanently ceased, no enforcement action can be taken.

4.2.5 Time limits and Lawful Development Certificates under section 191

An application may be made to the local planning authority, under section 191, to certify that an existing use, operation, or failure to comply with a condition or limitation is lawful. Most cases turn on the rules concerning time limits for immunity from enforcement action, so it is convenient to examine them here.

Established use rights arising under the old rules (a change of use before 1964) are not lost under the current rules, which were introduced by the *Planning and Compensation Act* 1991.

Panton v Secretary of State for the Environment, Transport and the Regions (1999)

P claimed that various uses had become immune from enforcement action because either they commenced before 1964, or they continued for ten years prior to the coming into effect of the new ten-year rule in July 1992, or they continued for a period of ten years prior to his application for a lawful development certificate in 1997. The inspector found that various uses existed from before 1964 to the 1980s but did not operate during the ten-year period up to the application for a certificate. She therefore found that those uses were no longer lawful.

The judge held that the inspector had erred. Where there was evidence of an accrued established use capable of giving rise to the right to an established use certificate under the pre-1992 rules, such a right could only be lost by abandonment, the formation of a new planning unit or by material change of use.

The relevant use, operation or non-compliance with a condition must subsist at the date of the application for the certificate.

In respect of an application relating to non-compliance with a condition, the non-compliance must have continued throughout a period of ten years.

Nicholson v Secretary of State for the Environment, Transport and the Regions (1998)

From 1984 to 1991 a dwelling was occupied in breach of an agricultural occupancy condition. In 1991 the dwelling was sold and remained unoccupied whilst various extensions and improvements were undertaken. An application for a certificate of lawfulness was made in 1995. This was refused and the owner appealed.

The judge held that, under the terms of section 191, an application for a certificate could only be made if there is non-compliance with the condition at the time. The applicant will then be entitled to a certificate if there has been a breach for the ten-year period. If it were otherwise, the breach of an occupancy condition for six months followed by compliance would mean a certificate could be issued after ten years. The judge distinguished non-compliance with a condition from the continuation or abandonment of a use. If non-compliance ceases, the breach is at an end but the condition continues in force. A subsequent non-compliance is a fresh breach and the ten-year period for enforcement starts again; it is not permissible to add the period of one breach to that of a subsequent separate breach.

An unauthorised seasonal use can become established (*Webber v Minister of Housing and Local Government* (1967)). However, seasonal occupation cannot achieve immunity from enforcement of an agricultural occupancy condition, as the breach of the condition does not continue when the property is unoccupied.

North Devon District Council v Secretary of State for the Environment, Transport and the Regions (1998)

In 1975 the appellants acquired a bungalow subject to an agricultural occupancy condition and let it out for holiday accommodation from May to September every year. It was unoccupied in the winter months. In 1990 they applied for a lawful development certificate for use as a holiday cottage without complying with the agricultural occupancy condition. It was claimed, following *Webber v Minister of Housing and Local Government*, that a seasonal use could become established if it occurred regularly every year. The Secretary of State agreed and the local authority appealed.

The judge distinguished the *Webber* case. That was not a case about a breach of condition, but about the material change of use of agricultural land to a campsite during the summer months over a number of years. The issue here was not about use but about breach of condition. During the winter months there was no breach of condition so enforcement action could not be taken. There had therefore been no continuous breach of the condition for ten years.

(The judge observed that continuous physical occupation is not required for there to be occupation in breach. It will be a matter of fact and degree whether breach continues despite absence for a time.)

Where a condition restricts occupation to periods of a year or to certain days of the week, does it mean that immunity can never be acquired by permanent occupation because the breach stops during each permitted period or day? Mr Justice Sullivan, in *North Devon v First Secretary of State*, said 'No'.

North Devon District Council v First Secretary of State (2004)

Planning permission had been granted in 1971 for five holiday bungalows subject to a condition that they should be occupied only from 15 March to 15 November in each year. The claimant had occupied one of the bungalows on a permanent basis since 1992 and applied for a lawful development certificate in 2002. Relying on the *Nicholson* and the *North Devon* (1998) cases, the council claimed that the breach was not for a continuous period of ten years as occupation was permitted every March to November. Mr Justice Sullivan distinguished these cases as neither was concerned with a seasonal occupancy condition. Statements in those cases about the need for a continuous breach, while appropriate where it is possible to have non-compliance throughout the year, are 'wholly inappropriate where

159

non-compliance throughout the year is impossible'. He stated that the council could have issued an enforcement notice after 14 March in any year in respect of the breach of condition over the previous winter, even though the occupation had ceased to be in breach. The judge derived support for this from the statement in the *Thurrock* case, above, that enforcement action can be taken although a breach has temporarily ceased.

4.2.6 Further enforcement action

Section 171B(4)(b) was added to enable enforcement action to be taken where the first attempt to enforce against the breach was technically defective and a second would have been out of time. Further enforcement action in respect of that breach can be taken within four years of the first purported action. It does not matter that the breach is wrongly described in the first notice so long as both notices address the same breach.

Jarmain v Secretary of State for the Environment, Transport and the Regions (1999)

Permission was granted for a mobile home subject to a condition that the permission expired on 31 March 1995. Over a period of time physical alterations to the mobile home had converted it into a permanent single-storey building by 12 April 1993. On 22 March 1996 the local authority served an enforcement notice alleging a breach of the time condition and requiring the removal of the mobile home. When the authority realised they had misdescribed the breach, they served a second notice, on 13 March 1998, alleging the erection of a building without planning permission. The appellant claimed that the local authority could not invoke section 171B(4)(b) because the breach in the second notice (erection of a building) was not the same as the first (breach of condition), so the second notice was out of time.

The judge held that so long as the actual breach of development control is the same it does not matter that it is described in different ways. The local authority's mistake did not change the nature of the breach and it was plain that both notices were aimed at the construction of a permanent dwellinghouse.

4.3 ISSUE OF ENFORCEMENT NOTICE – SECTION 172

The local planning authority may issue an enforcement notice where it appears to them that there has been a breach of planning control and that it is expedient to do so, having regard to the development plan and any other material considerations.

4.3.1 The decision to issue a notice

There is no duty on the local planning authority to investigate whether the developer could bring himself within some exemption.

Tidswell v Secretary of State for the Environment and Thurrock Borough Council (1977)

Enforcement action was taken in respect of a Sunday market that had operated on nine Sundays. The applicant challenged the validity of the notice on the ground that there was no breach of planning control, because use for a market for no more than 14 days in a calendar year is permitted development (see Chapter 2).

It was held that it was not for the local planning authority to investigate to decide whether the developer could bring himself within some exemption or permission. There was evidence that the use was permanent, so the authority were entitled to take the view that there had been a breach.

The planning authority cannot resolve to issue an enforcement notice in the expectation of a future breach if it appears that there has yet been no breach.

R v Rochester upon Medway City Council, ex parte Hobday (1989)

The applicant had used a site for market purposes. The planning authority resolved that on or after the 15th day of market use, an enforcement notice be issued together with a stop notice (because at that time the authority had not taken account of the fact that the use might be permanent as in *Tidswell*).

It was held that the enforcement subsequently issued on this basis was a nullity, because the 1990 Act requires consideration of past or present, but not prospective, breaches of planning control.

Although the decision whether to issue an enforcement notice is a matter for the discretion of the local authority, the court may grant an application for judicial review where the decision not to enforce is on a false basis.

R v Sevenoaks District Council, ex parte Palley (1994)

An application to determine whether a glasshouse needed prior approval was made in 1992. If it was on land comprised in an agricultural unit it would be permitted development unless it was within 25 metres of a classified road. When it transpired that the proposed glasshouse was not within 25 metres of a road the authority required no further details. A glasshouse was erected in 1994. A neighbouring landowner claimed that the land was not agricultural but the local authority refused to take enforcement action. The neighbour sought judicial review.

Mr Justice Tucker found that the question whether land was in use for agriculture was not likely to be a straightforward paper inquiry and might require site inspections, etc. As the council gave the most cursory attention to the question, the decision not to take enforcement action proceeded on a false basis.

A local planning authority cannot bind itself not to exercise its enforcement powers. Nor can it be 'estopped' from taking enforcement action, although in certain circumstances there might be a 'legitimate expectation' that a development may be treated as lawful. See *Henry Boot Homes Ltd v Bassetlaw District Council* (2002), at 2.2.1.

4.3.2 Service of notice

Section 172(2) provides that a copy of the notice shall be served on the owner and the occupier of the land to which it relates and on any other person having an interest in the land, being an interest which, in the opinion of the authority, is materially affected by the notice.

Owner

Owner is defined in section 336(1) as 'the person, other than a mortgagee not in possession, who, whether in his own right or as trustee for any person, is entitled to receive the rack rent or, where the land is not let at a rack rent, would be so entitled if it were so let'.

London Corporation v Cusack-Smith (1955)

Owner, as defined in section 336, was held by the House of Lords not to include a freeholder who actually has let land at less than a rack rent. In such a case the tenant will be regarded as the owner.

Occupier

An occupier may include a licensee. Whether a person is an occupier is a matter of fact and degree.

Stevens v Bromley London Borough Council (1972)

The issue in this case was whether a licensee of a pitch on an unauthorised caravan site was an 'occupier'. The Court of Appeal held that it is a question of fact and degree in each case. There were 10 or 11 large caravans on the site. They had mains water and electricity, and drains connected each caravan to a common cesspool. Many had gardens with the boundary of the plot marked off with rocks. Rent was paid weekly and a licence could not be revoked without one month's written notice. The caravans were the licensees' permanent homes. In the circumstances, the licensee was an occupier.

> 'No one, except, perhaps, a lawyer could doubt that he was in occupation of that land.' (Lord Justice Salmon)

An occupier may include a trespasser. (But note that section 179(4) restricts liability to a person 'who has control of or an interest in the land to which the enforcement notice relates'.)

Scarborough Borough Council v Adams and Adams (1983)

Enforcement notices were served in respect of caravans parked in a lay-by owned by the Highway Authority. The caravans were apparently permanent homes. Following *Stevens v Bromley London Borough Council*, the Divisional Court held that there may be circumstances where squatters can be regarded as occupiers for the purposes of planning legislation. It depended on such factors as the length of time they had been on the site and the use to which the site had been put. In the circumstances the squatters were occupiers.

Person having an interest in the land

An 'interest in the land' means a legal or equitable interest (*Stevens v Bromley London Borough Council*) and does not include licensees.

4.3.3 Date and mode of service

Service shall take place not more than 28 days after the date of issue and not less than 28 days before the date on which the notice comes into effect – section 172(3).

Section 329 gives various modes of service to enable an authority to effectively serve any notice or document under the 1990 Act. (See *Morecambe and Heysham Corporation v Warwick* (1958) as to personal delivery.)

4.4 CONTENTS AND EFFECT OF NOTICE – SECTION 173

The statutory requirements for an enforcement notice are set out in section 173. The key provisions are, broadly, as follows.

4.4.1 Section 173(1) – matters to be stated

'An enforcement notice shall state:

(a) the matters which appear to the local planning authority to constitute the breach of planning control; and

(b) the paragraph of section 171A(1) within which, in the opinion of the authority, the breach falls.' (See 4.1.)

4.4.2 Section 173(2) – compliance with section 173(1)(a)

'A notice complies with section 173(1)(a) if it enables any person on whom a copy of it is served to know what those matters are.'

This is a statutory formulation of part of the classic test set out in *Miller-Mead v Minister of Housing and Local Government* (1963) by Lord Justice Upjohn:

'... in my judgment, the test must be: does the notice tell him fairly what he has done wrong and what he must do to remedy it?' (See 4.5.)

4.4.3 Section 173(3) – steps to be specified

'An enforcement notice shall specify the steps which the authority require to be taken, or the activities which the authority require to cease, in order to achieve, wholly or partly, the following purposes.'

4.4.4 Section 173(4) – purposes behind the notice – remedies

'Those purposes are:

(a)   remedying the breach by making any development comply with the terms (including conditions and limitations) of any planning permission which has been granted in respect of the land, by discontinuing any use of the land or by restoring land to its condition before the breach took place; or

(b)   remedying any injury to amenity caused by the breach.'

Parts (a) and (b) of section 174 are not 'fully disjunctive'. In other words, steps required to be taken may include a mixture of (a) and (b).

Wyatt Brothers (Oxford) Ltd v Secretary of State for the Environment, Transport and the Regions (2001)

'Bearing in mind that the words "wholly or partly" in section 173(3) expressly enabled the local planning authority to "under enforce" it is not difficult to envisage circumstances in which a local planning authority might want to require in one enforcement notice a partial restoration of the status quo coupled with other work designed to remedy the injury to amenity caused by the breach.' (Lord Justice Kennedy.)

4.4.5 Section 173(8) – date the notice takes effect

'An enforcement notice shall specify the date on which it is to take effect ...'

4.4.6 Section 173(9) – time for compliance

An enforcement notice shall specify the period at the end of which any steps are required to have been taken or any activities ceased (and may specify different periods for different steps and activities).

R (on the application of Lynes) v West Berkshire District Council (2003)

Enforcement notices were served in connection with the use of land for human burial without planning permission. Each notice stated the date it took effect, and also stated that the time for compliance was 'immediately this notice takes effect'. Mr Justice Harrison held that a period of compliance cannot start before the notice comes into effect, therefore there was no period of compliance as required by the 1990 Act. The notice was therefore a nullity, as it did not comply with the statutory requirements for a valid notice.

4.4.7 Section 173(10) – prescribed information

An enforcement notice shall specify such additional matters as may be prescribed. See the appropriate regulations – SI 2002/2682 (England) and SI 2003/394 (Wales).

4.4.8 Section 173(11) – under enforcement and deemed planning permission

If the planning authority decides to under enforce in relation to the breach alleged in the notice (see section 173(3) above), then so long as the notice is complied with, planning permission is deemed to have been granted under section 73A (retrospective permission) for the operations and activities which were not enforced against.

Section 173(11) does not grant permission in respect of a breach or breaches not identified in the enforcement notice.

Fidler v First Secretary of State (2004)

The site was used for a mixture of purposes including agriculture, storage, haulage depot, a building and demolition contractor's depot, motor vehicle repairs, etc. An enforcement notice was served which, in effect, required the cessation of the non-agricultural uses. This notice was upheld. However, an earlier notice was directed at use of part of the site as an engineering contractor's depot. The notice required cessation of this use and the removal of equipment in connection with it. It was therefore claimed that this was a case of under enforcement and all the other activities (not mentioned in that notice) had deemed planning permission,

The Court of Appeal rejected this claim. It was held, following *Scott v Secretary of State for the Environment* (2000), that section 173(11) only applies to activities that are included in the description of the breach in the notice.

Where there are mixed uses in breach of planning control, it is a question of fact and degree whether this constitutes a single breach or a number of separate breaches (*Tandridge District Council v Verrechia* (1999)). If there is a single breach, then all the components of that breach should be alleged. If not, then the principles in *Scott* and *Fidler* apply.

To fall within section 173(11) the notice must set out some steps to remedy the breach. An enforcement notice which requires no steps at all could not properly be described as an 'enforcement' notice for section 173 purposes.

Tandridge District Council v Verrechia (1999)

The appellant owned land that he used for the dumping of waste materials and for the commercial parking of cars. The county planning authority served an enforcement notice in respect of the waste and a planning inspector purported to correct the notice to add the parking breach, but set out no remedial steps. So the appellant claimed that car parking now had planning permission by virtue of section 173(11).

The Court of Appeal held that a notice could under enforce, but it could not fail to enforce at all. The amendment was ineffective and section 173(11) could not apply. The Court also held that the mixed use consisted of two separate uses and the inspector was purporting to add a new and separate breach.

4.5 NULLITY AND INVALIDITY

So long as the notice complies with the statutory requirements it is not a nullity, although it may be invalid in that it can be quashed on appeal because, for example, no permission is required for the activity enforced against. The distinction between nullity and invalidity is not always easy to discern. A nullity cannot be amended.

Miller-Mead v Minister of Housing and Local Government (1963)

An enforcement notice required the removal of caravans. M-M contended that the notice was defective as he had existing use rights for the parking and storage of caravans for repair and sale. On appeal, the Minister varied the notice by inserting the word 'residential' before the word 'caravans' and changed the remedy to require the removal of caravans used for human habitation. M-M challenged this decision, in effect claiming that the notice, being a nullity, could not be amended.

The Court of Appeal held that the notice was not a nullity and the Minister had acted within his powers. The Court observed that a planning authority cannot necessarily know all the relevant facts and may serve a notice where there 'appears' to be a breach.

Lord Justice Upjohn stated that a notice is a nullity if it does not comply with the mandatory statutory requirements. So if it fails to specify the steps to remedy the breach, or the date it comes into effect, or the period for compliance, it will be a nullity. He also stated that a notice which is hopelessly ambiguous and uncertain would be a nullity. But if development without permission is alleged and it is found that no permission is required, the notice is invalid and can be quashed on appeal; it is not a nullity. It is the same where a breach of condition has been alleged but the condition has been complied with. The notice in question alleged a breach greater than that which was established; this error was not fatal to the notice.

Alleging the wrong category of breach used to be regarded as rendering the notice a nullity (e.g. material change of use instead of breach of condition). This is no longer the case so long as the notice can be amended without injustice – see for example the *Ahern* case below.

R v Secretary of State for the Environment, ex parte Ahern (London) Ltd (1989)

Planning permission for use of land as a skip transfer waste station was granted subject to a condition that the use cease by 31 August 1987. In September an enforcement notice was served alleging a material change of use. It was common ground that it should have cited breach of condition. On appeal the inspector determined that the notice was so defective as to be a nullity. The applicants challenged that decision in the High Court.

Mr Justice Roch held that the notice was not a nullity and could be varied by the Secretary of State under his powers in the 1990 Act, as the variation would be without injustice to the appellant or the local planning authority. He stated that the law has progressed:

'to the point where the pettifogging has stopped, where artificial and nice distinctions understood only by lawyers no longer prevail, and the Act can be read so that it means what it says ...'

He held that it was no longer the case that stating the wrong breach was an error that could not be corrected, as the earlier cases showed. The statement of Lord Denning in *Miller-Mead* (above) that the Minister 'can correct errors so long as, having regard to the merits of the case, the correction can be made without injustice' is the law.

A notice which is 'hopelessly ambiguous', in the words of Lord Justice Upjohn in *Miller-Mead*, is a nullity.

Metallic Protectives Ltd v Secretary of State for the Environment (1976)

Planning permission had been granted subject to a condition that no nuisance should be caused by reason of the emission of noise, etc. An enforcement notice was served requiring the occupier to install 'satisfactory soundproofing' of a compressor. The Secretary of State accepted that the wording was too vague and modified it to include decibel measures and other specific steps.

The Divisional Court held that the notice was so vague that it did not comply with the statutory requirement to specify the steps required to remedy the breach. It did not indicate a point at which the occupiers could be certain they had complied with the notice. The notice was therefore a nullity incapable of amendment.

Dudley Bowers Amusements Enterprises Ltd v Secretary of State for the Environment (1986)

A Sunday market had been held in Cleethorpes from March to September in 1983. In 1984 an enforcement notice requiring markets and associated car parking not to be held 'on such Sundays which fall within the period of summer time in any year' was amended by the inspector by including a reference to the *Summer Time Act* 1972. The judge held that the wording of the notice was so hopelessly ambiguous as to render it a nullity. So it could not be amended.

A notice that does not set out a period of compliance is a nullity, as it does not comply with the requirements of the 1990 Act. See *R (on the application of Lynes)* (2003) above.

Matters of fact and degree may be incorporated in a notice in appropriate cases without rendering the notice a nullity.

R v Runnymede Borough Council, ex parte Sarvan Singh (1987)

An enforcement notice required religious purposes, other than those incidental to the enjoyment of the dwellinghouse, to cease. The applicant claimed that the notice was imprecise and so void.

Mr Justice Schiemann stated that it was admissible to use wording which incorporated matters of fact and degree. The recipient is then left with making a judgment on how to behave.

4.6 ENFORCEMENT AND THE PLANNING UNIT

It has been seen that it is necessary to establish what the planning unit is in order to determine whether there has been a material change of use (see 1.7.7). But this does not mean that the planning unit must be identified in an enforcement notice. The planning authority may bring enforcement proceedings in respect of the whole planning unit or in respect of some smaller portion on which the breach occurs.

Hawkey v Secretary of State for the Environment (1971)

The site consisted of a haulage contractor's yard on which there stood a bungalow, a workshop and five other small buildings. An office and a canteen in the bungalow were used in connection with the business in the yard. The appellant began to repair vehicles other than his own and to carry out a car hire service. An enforcement notice against these uses was served in respect of the yard but not the bungalow. The appellant claimed that the notice should have been directed to the planning unit, that is the yard plus bungalow.

The Divisional Court held that an enforcement notice need not identify the planning unit. It may, as in this case, be directed to the area where the unlawful activity is taking place. It is open to the landowner to try to establish, on appeal, that the planning unit is larger than that specified in the notice and that therefore no material change of use has taken place.

Morris v Secretary of State for the Environment (1975)

The appellant operated a motor sales and service business on the northern half of a five acre site. The southern half was used for fruit growing. The planning authority served an enforcement notice requiring the motor business to cease. The notice was served in respect of the whole site. It was contended that the notice should have been restricted in its effect to that part of the premises on which the motor business was actually carried on.

The Divisional Court upheld the notice. Once enforcement action has become possible because there has been a material change in the use of the whole unit, the planning authority should be entitled to enforce against the whole unit.

The enforcement notice does not conclusively identify the planning unit.

Burdle v Secretary of State for the Environment (1972)

'... what I cannot accept is that the accident of language which the planning authority choose to use in framing their enforcement notice can determine conclusively what is the appropriate planning unit ...' (Mr Justice Bridge)

It is legitimate to issue several enforcement notices in relation to the same site so long as the effect is not to restrict the landowner's rights unjustifiably (*de Mulder v Secretary of State for the Environment* (1974)). Nor does it matter that the notices overlap or relate to the same activity.

Ramsey v Secretary of State for the Environment (1991)

R owned a farm of 112 hectares. Within the farm was a site, Suffolk Motopark, operated by RS Ltd, a company owned by R. The planning authority served an enforcement notice in respect of Suffolk Motopark requiring vehicular activity to cease. The authority also served an enforcement notice in respect of the whole farm, for they feared that if they did not, the vehicular activity would simply be moved from one part of the farm to another. It was claimed that the notice in respect of the whole farm was void as it was not lawful to issue two notices in relation to two sites, one of which overlaps or includes the other. The judge held that the notice was valid. However he observed that it would be unjustified to prosecute under both notices for the same breach.

In an appropriate case an enforcement notice may be served in respect of more than one plot of land under separate ownership or occupation. If this were to cause prejudice, the inspector would have the power to vary the notice.

Rawlins v Secretary of State for the Environment (1990)

Travelling showmen and their families had placed caravans, fairground rides and equipment, machinery and vehicles upon agricultural land in the green belt. A road and hardstandings had been constructed. The planning authority served enforcement notices, each of which related to the site as one unit. The development had been carried out as a concerted whole and was in common ownership until individual plots were sold at the time of the enforcement notices. Many of the plots remained undivided and not clearly defined. The notices were challenged on the ground that they were not served on the 'owner and occupier of the land' (i.e. each plot) as required by the 1990 Act.

The Court of Appeal dismissed the challenge. The case had exceptional features which justified the less usual procedure adopted. The Court was not setting aside the existing long-established practice of issuing enforcement notices on a planning unit. If there was a possibility of injustice an inspector would have power to vary the notice, split it up or even exclude the land of the affected occupier altogether.

4.7   THE MANSI PRINCIPLE

An enforcement notice cannot take away legally permitted rights such as existing use rights. The notice should be amended to make it clear that it does not prohibit lawful uses.

Mansi v Elstree Rural District Council (1964)

Since 1922, the appeal site had been used primarily for horticulture with a secondary use for retail sale of nursery produce and some imported fruit and vegetables. In 1959

M acquired the site and began to use one of the greenhouses and a concrete area in front of it, upon which he placed a stall, for the sale of goods, including drinks and ice-cream. An enforcement notice was served requiring the sale of goods to be discontinued. M claimed that the notice went too far in that it was an embargo on all sales of goods and would prevent him from continuing the limited retail sales which had been a feature of the site for 40 years.

The Divisional Court agreed.

'The planning Acts gave no power to the local planning authority to restrict or remove that use, such as it was.' (Mr Justice Widgery)

Following *Miller-Mead v MHLG* (above) the notice was not a nullity, but the Minister should have recognised that it went too far and he ought to have amended it to make it clear that it did not prevent retail use on the scale and in the manner which was lawful.

It is not strictly necessary for the inspector or Secretary of State to amend an enforcement notice to save an ancillary use. There is no need to specify the obvious. And there is absolutely no need at all to refer to the appellant's permitted development rights under the GPDO.

R v Harfield (1993)

A petrol station had been used for the parking of commercial vehicles and the storage of scrap metal and scrap vehicle parts. An enforcement notice was served requiring discontinuance of the unauthorised parking and scrap uses and removal of all commercial vehicles and scrap. The owner was prosecuted for non-compliance with the notice. At the trial he was not allowed to lead evidence that the parking of commercial vehicles was ancillary to the petrol station use and so was convicted because, by his own admission, he had not removed all the commercial vehicles.

The Court of Appeal quashed the conviction. According to the *Mansi* principle no enforcement notice can take away legally permitted rights and the authorities clearly established that any enforcement notice would be construed so as to retain any such rights. Therefore the enforcement must be read as meaning the parking of commercial vehicles which cannot be described as ancillary.

Duguid v Secretary of State for the Environment, Transport and the Regions (2000)

An enforcement notice was issued to stop the use of an airfield for the holding of markets and car boot sales. The notice was upheld on appeal.

D appealed to the High Court claiming that the enforcement notice should have been amended to preserve his rights under the GPDO to hold markets for not more than 14 days in any calendar year.

The Court of Appeal dismissed the appeal. The notice cannot be construed so as to make a criminal offence out of a lawful activity permitted by the GPDO. There is no need at all to refer to the GPDO in the notice because it operates as a matter of law. By contrast, in a case like *Mansi* it makes good sense for the notice to be amended to safeguard the established right and to avoid any future argument as to its extent.

Note that section 173(5)(c) provides that a notice may require any activity not to be carried on except to the extent specified in the notice. In a complex case where there had been a history of mixed and fluctuating uses, Lord Justice Carnwath observed that the burden is on the appellant to propose, under ground (f), limits to his activities which are acceptable to the planning authority – *Fidler v First Secretary of State* (2004). See also *Taylor & Sons (Farms) v Secretary of State for the Environment* (2002) at 4.9.2 below.

4.8 APPEAL AGAINST ENFORCEMENT NOTICE

Where an appeal is brought, the enforcement notice is of no effect, subject to an order under section 289(4A), pending the final determination or the withdrawal of the appeal – section 175(4).

Section 289 allows an appeal to the High Court (with leave) from a decision of the Secretary of State on a point of law. Section 289(4A) allows the Court to order that the notice has effect pending the final determination in order to defeat those who abuse the appeal process to buy more time.

4.8.1 Who may appeal?

A person having an interest in the land to which an enforcement notice relates or a 'relevant occupier' may appeal to the Secretary of State, whether or not a copy of it has been served on him – section 174(1).

'Relevant occupier' means a person who, on the date of issue of the notice, occupies the land by virtue of a licence and continues so to occupy when the appeal is brought – section 174(6). So a trespasser has no right of appeal. But he may, of course, apply for planning permission and appeal against refusal.

R v Secretary of State for the Environment, ex parte Davis (1989)

A gypsy resided in a caravan at a quarry. She received an enforcement notice requiring the caravan's removal. The Secretary of State determined that her appeal against the notice was invalid, as she was a trespasser. She claimed that this decision was a denial of her human rights.

Mr Justice McCowan determined that, as a trespasser can apply for planning permission and appeal against a refusal, there was no substance in this claim. She could by such means challenge the planning merits of the decision.

The interest in land must subsist at the time the appeal is brought but there is no requirement that it subsisted when the notice was issued. However, a 'relevant occupier' must establish a licence both at the date of issue and the date of appeal.

R v Secretary of State for the Environment, Transport and the Regions, ex parte Benham-Crosswell (2001)

The appellants were tenants of agricultural land under a lease expiring on 28 October 1998. The lease excluded the operation of the *Agricultural Holdings Act* 1986, so no yearly tenancy arose on expiry. An enforcement notice, dated 13 October 1998, was served in respect of engineering operations. The appellants lodged appeals which were received on 18 November 1998. No new tenancy or licence was granted to the appellants and the inspector found no evidence to support the appellants' claims that implied licences had been granted.

It was held that the appellants had no right to appeal. Although they had an interest in land at the date of issue of the notice, they had no such interest (i.e. a legal or equitable interest) at the date the appeal was brought, namely when it was received on 18 November. Furthermore, a 'relevant occupier' must establish a licence both at the date of issue and the date of appeal.

4.8.2 Grounds of appeal – section 174(2)

(a) Planning permission ought to be granted or a condition or limitation discharged.

(b) The matters stated in the notice have not occurred.

(c) Those matters, if they occurred, do not constitute a breach of planning control.

(d) At the date the notice was issued no enforcement action could be taken. (See 4.2.)

(e) Copies of the notice were not served as required. (The fact that a person was not served may be disregarded if neither the appellant nor that person was substantially prejudiced – section 176(5).)

(f) The remedy required is excessive.

(Note on ground f: It may be advisable for the appellant to submit a fall-back position to the inspector. See *Taylor & Sons (Farms) v Secretary of State for the Environment*, at 4.9.2 below.)

(g) The period for compliance is too short.

4.8.3 Notice of appeal

Section 174(3) provides for various forms of service of notice of appeal. It must be given, delivered or transmitted before the enforcement notice takes effect.

The time limit for making an appeal is absolute.

Howard v Secretary of State for the Environment (1975)

The appellant's original notice of appeal did not state the grounds relied upon and so a subsequent letter was drafted setting out the grounds. This letter was drafted two days before the expiry of the enforcement notice but, by mischance, was not posted for another four days and so arrived after the expiry date.

The Court of Appeal held that it was imperative to comply with the time limit, otherwise the machinery of enforcement would not work.

(The current provisions require that a written statement of the grounds, including a brief statement of the facts, must be set out in the notice of appeal or provided within 14 days from the date on which the Secretary of State sends a notice requiring such a statement. See section 174(4) of the Act and SI 2002/2682 (England) and SI 2003/394 (Wales).)

Service of notice of appeal

As the appeal must be given before the enforcement notice takes effect, care must be taken if the date the notice takes effect is the day after a Sunday, Saturday or Bank Holiday, because there may be difficulties effecting delivery on a non-working day. However, if there is a letterbox or other channel of communication which can be used on that day, the notice of appeal can be successfully given.

R v Secretary of State for the Environment, ex parte JBI Financial Consultants (1989)

An enforcement notice came into effect on 1 June 1987, a Monday. The notice of appeal was delivered by hand on that day. The Secretary of State declined to deal with the appeal as it had been given one day too late. The claimant contended that delivery could not have been effected on the Sunday as the offices were closed, so the appeal should have been accepted.

Mr Justice Henry rejected this contention. The appeal could have been properly given by posting it through the letterbox.

'The presence of a letterbox is in itself a holding out that documents put through the letterbox will be treated as having been received inside and so would, for the purpose of this case, be the giving of the notice for the making of the appeal.'

Burden and standard of proof in enforcement appeals

The burden of proving relevant facts is upon the appellant. The standard of proof is the balance of probability.

Nelsovil v Minister of Housing and Local Government (1962)

An enforcement notice was served in respect of use of premises as a club. The appellant claimed that he had established use rights. The Minister was not satisfied on the evidence that there were such use rights. The appellant contended that the onus is on the local planning authority to establish the facts upon which an enforcement notice is based, and that there was no evidence upon which the Minister could decide that the appeal premises had no established use rights as a club.

The Divisional Court rejected this. A person given a right to appeal on certain specified grounds is the person who has to make good those grounds and is the person on whom that onus rests.

Thrasyvoulou v Secretary of State for the Environment and Hackney London Borough Council (1984)

In his decision letter, a planning inspector concluded that he was not satisfied that there was sufficient evidence to show 'beyond all reasonable doubt' that the appeal property had remained in use as a guest house over the relevant period. So he upheld the notice.

The High Court held that the standard of proof is the civil standard of the balance of probability. The use of the phrase 'beyond reasonable doubt' was the criminal standard and so the decision would be set aside.

4.9 CORRECTION AND VARIATION OF NOTICES BY SECRETARY OF STATE

4.9.1 Powers under section 176(1)

'On an appeal under section 174 the Secretary of State may:

(a) correct any defect, error or misdescription in the enforcement notice; or

(b) vary the terms of the enforcement notice,

if he is satisfied that the correction or variation will not cause injustice to the appellant or the local planning authority.'

The proviso to these paragraphs brings the statute clearly into line with Lord Denning's statement in *Miller-Mead* that errors can be corrected if they can be made without injustice. The same test is now applied to variations.

It has already been seen that significant errors can be corrected, such as alleging the wrong category of breach as in *R v Secretary of State for the Environment, ex parte Ahern* (1989). But an error that renders the notice a nullity cannot be amended.

A correction may narrow the scope of the notice and even broaden its scope, provided there is no injustice to the appellant. It is a question of fact for the Secretary of State or the inspector. The courts are not prepared to write artificial restrictions into the power to vary or correct.

Hammond v Secretary of State for the Environment and Maldon District Council (1997)

A mobile home on a smallholding was used for residential purposes. An enforcement notice alleged that the breach was 'the stationing of a mobile home'. It had been established in *Wealden District Council v Secretary of State for the Environment* (1988) that stationing a caravan on agricultural land was not development where the caravan was ancillary to the agricultural use. So the inspector corrected the allegation in the notice to 'the stationing of a mobile home for the purpose of human habitation'.

The Court of Appeal upheld the correction. The appellant knew perfectly well what the mobile home was being used for and what the local authority was complaining about. Lord Justice Brooke completely agreed with Mr Justice Roch in *R v Secretary of State for the Environment, ex parte Ahern* that the pettifogging has stopped and the 1990 Act can be read so that when it says the Secretary of State can correct *any* defect, if it can be made without injustice, it means exactly that.

Lynch v Secretary of State for the Environment, Transport and the Regions (1999)

The judge held that it did not follow that injustice would necessarily be caused by a widening of the terms of the notice. Whether injustice would be caused is a matter for the inspector and the appellant had failed to establish that no reasonable inspector would have ordered the amendments.

The power to correct or vary does not allow an addition to a local planning authority's enforcement notice which could not have been included in the first place. Nor can a power to vary include the addition of a breach without specifying any steps by way of remedy.

Tandridge District Council v Verrechia (1999)

Land was used for waste disposal and for car parking. Neither use had planning permission. The district council served an enforcement notice in respect of car parking and the county council subsequently served an enforcement notice in respect of the waste – a county matter. The inspector purported to amend the county's notice to include the car parking, but included no remedy.

The Court of Appeal held that, as the notice remains that of the local authority (it was not a Secretary of State's enforcement notice under section 182) it was not permissible for the inspector to add anything which the local authority could not have included in the first place. Nor can a breach be added without a remedy.

4.9.2 Variation and ground (f)

In an appeal on ground (f) it may be advisable to submit a fallback position and indicate what variation to the notice should be made.

Taylor & Sons (Farms) v Secretary of State for the Environment, Transport and the Regions (2001)

The appellant constructed a large hardstanding on his farm without planning permission. An enforcement notice was served requiring the removal of the hardstanding and the appellant appealed by written representations on various grounds including ground (f). The notices were upheld on appeal.

The appellant claimed that the inspector should have varied the notice so as to leave that much of the hardstanding as was reasonably necessary for the purposes of agriculture and therefore permitted development within the GPDO. If there was no material before her upon which to decide which area to choose, she should have asked for further submissions.

The Court of Appeal held that appellant should contemplate the possibility of failure in the appeal (appealing on ground (f) shows this is the position). If there is a fallback position it should be made clear in the submissions. The appellant was professionally advised and the advisers had chosen not to make any submissions in detail under ground (f). In these circumstances any failure by the inspector to advert in her decision letter to the possibility of asking for further submissions did not amount to an error of law.

4.10 NON-COMPLIANCE WITH ENFORCEMENT NOTICE

It is a criminal offence to fail to comply with an enforcement notice.

4.10.1 The 'owner' offence

Section 179(1)

'Where, at any time after the end of the period for compliance with an enforcement notice, any step required by the notice to be taken has not been taken or any activity required by the notice to cease is being carried on, the person who is then the owner of the land is in breach of the notice.'

Section 179(2)

'Where the owner of the land is in breach of an enforcement notice he shall be guilty of an offence.'

Owner is defined in section 336(1) as 'the person, other than a mortgagee not in possession, who, whether in his own right or as trustee for any person, is entitled to receive the rack rent or, where the land is not let at a rack rent, would be so entitled if it were so let'. (See 4.3.2.)

It is for the local authority to prove, beyond reasonable doubt, that the defendant is the owner at the relevant time. What is sufficient to establish ownership depends on the facts and circumstances of the case.

Walton v Sedgefield Borough Council (1999)

Mr Walton was prosecuted by the local authority for not complying with an enforcement notice. He claimed that the prosecution had not proved that he was the owner of the land at the material time. The evidence upon which the justices relied was an application by Walton for a lawful use certificate, on which he had described himself as the owner, and letters from his solicitor which used terms indicating that he was the owner.

The defence submitted that it is necessary in every case to prove who receives or is capable of receiving the rack rent. The Divisional Court rejected this. What is sufficient to establish ownership depends on the circumstances of the case. There was nothing in this case to suggest any complexity of interests in the land. The certificate and letters were admissible evidence which provided prima facie evidence of ownership to the criminal standard of proof.

Where there is a transfer of title but the purchaser has not yet become the registered proprietor, the vendor is still the owner within the definition in section 336(1). The purchaser may also be prosecuted if he is a person in control of the land (below, section 179(4)). Whether the vendor would have the defence of not being able to secure compliance is considered below.

East Lindsey District Council v Thompson (2001)

During the compliance period of an enforcement notice, the owner sold the land. The transfer was not registered until 16 months later. The vendor was prosecuted for non-compliance and claimed that he was no longer the owner. The Divisional Court held that he was, as he was still the registered proprietor, entitled to receive the rack rent as trustee, at the relevant time. Lord Justice Keene observed that if a planning authority were not able to rely on the register they would have repeated difficulties when seeking to enforce.

4.10.2 Owner's defence under section 179(3)

'In proceedings against any person for an offence under [section 179(2)], it shall be a defence for him to show that he did everything he could be expected to do to secure compliance with the notice.'

It is implicit that there is an objective test to this defence. In other words, the owner must show that he did everything he could be reasonably expected to do.

R v Beard (John) (1997)

A gypsy was convicted of failing to comply with an enforcement notice on land that he owned. He appealed on the ground that he had a defence under section 179(3) in that he had searched for alternative accommodation without success and if forced to comply he would not be able to follow the traditional lifestyle of a gypsy. He also raised the matter of breach of Article 8 of the *European Convention on Human Rights* (see Chapter 3).

The Court of Appeal upheld the conviction. The defendant was physically capable of removing, or arranging the removal of, the hardstanding and caravans on the site. There was no conflict with the Convention, because the legitimate rights and expectations of gypsies are taken into account during the enforcement appeal process.

The passing of the *Human Rights Act* 1998 did not undermine *Beard*. Human rights issues are dealt with during the planning appeal process and are unsuitable matters for a criminal court.

R v Thomas George Clarke (2002)

A Romany gypsy pleaded the defence under section 179(3). He claimed he had nowhere else to station his caravan and he could not reasonably be expected to choose between abandoning his traditional gypsy way of life and evicting his family from the land and moving his caravan on to the roadside so as to comply with the enforcement notice.

The Court of Appeal followed *Beard* and held that this is no defence. There is no conflict with human rights because these issues had already been dealt with in the planning appeal process.

The court must take account of personal circumstances which may incapacitate the owner, but should be rigorous in the proof it demands from the defendant.

Kent County Council v Brockman (1996)

A 65-year-old man who had had a heart attack and was in difficult financial circumstances was unable to comply with an enforcement notice relating to land that he owned. The Divisional Court held that the magistrates may take personal circumstances into account in considering whether an owner has a defence under section 179(3). So a person who is genuinely incapacitated by reason of physical or financial incapacity has a defence. However, the judges sounded a note of caution about accepting protestations of impecuniosity. Lord Justice Simon Brown said that land should not be left in an unsatisfactory state unless a landowner has taken every practical step to overcome his financial problems in complying with the enforcement notice, to the extent if need be of selling his land.

Where the owner has sold the land, but the transfer has not yet been registered, he remains the legal owner. However, he may have a defence under section 179(3). It is a question of fact.

Thompson v East Lindsey District Council (2002)

After selling the land but before registration of title, Thompson was prosecuted for non-compliance with an enforcement notice. He was convicted and he appealed on the ground that, having established a bona fide sale, he had made out the defence in section 179(3).

That was not sufficient, said Mr Justice Richards. The court is entitled to look at other circumstances, such as the terms of the agreement between vendor and purchaser to see whether one or the other has accepted responsibility.

He observed that the defence is not just a defence of reasonable excuse; the defendant must prove, on the balance of probabilities, that he has done everything that he could be expected to do to secure compliance. In this case, Thompson had made an application for planning permission after the sale, and had not communicated to the purchaser in writing any request in respect of the non-compliance. The conclusion that he had not done everything that could have been expected was a finding that was reasonably open to the court on the facts.

4.10.3 The non-owner offence

Section 179(4)

'A person who has control of or an interest in the land to which an enforcement notice relates (other than the owner) must not carry on any activity which is required by the notice to cease or cause or permit such an activity to be carried on.'

Section 179(5)

'A person who, at any time after the end of the period for compliance with the notice, contravenes [section 179(4)] shall be guilty of an offence.'

(Note the defences for non-service under sections 179(7) and 285(2), which are available to both owners and non-owners.)

The word 'permit' was examined by the courts in the context of the pre-1991 law, under which it was an offence to cause or permit the use of land in breach of an enforcement notice. The prosecution must prove that the defendant had power to prevent the act and failed to take reasonable steps to prevent it.

Ragsdale v Creswick (1984)

An itinerant caravan dweller placed his caravan on land owned by the defendant and without his consent. Enforcement action was taken against the trespasser and the defendant. The defendant asked the trespasser to leave and sought advice and assistance from various agencies including the police, the council, the parish council, social services and his MP. However he did not apply to the court for an eviction order. The magistrates acquitted him and the matter came before the Divisional Court by way of case stated. The issue for the Divisional Court was, in essence, whether the failure to take legal proceedings meant that the defendant had failed to take reasonable steps to stop the trespasser using the land in breach of the notice.

The Court held that it is a question of fact. In the circumstances of the case there was sufficient material entitling the magistrates to acquit. Much depends on the nature of the proceedings, the prospects of success, the prospective cost and the prospects of the local authority succeeding in their action against the trespasser.

4.10.4 Defending a prosecution on grounds of invalidity

Section 285(1)

'The validity of an enforcement notice shall not, except by way of an appeal under Part VII, be questioned in any proceedings whatsoever on any of the grounds on which such an appeal may be brought.'

(These are the seven grounds set out in section 174 above).

Vale of White Horse District Council v Treble-Parker (1996)

The respondents had been prosecuted for non-compliance with an enforcement notice. The magistrates had allowed evidence that the change of use had begun more than ten years before the service of the enforcement notice and acquitted the respondents. The Divisional Court set aside the acquittal and remitted the case to the magistrates. The proper remedy was to appeal on ground (d) in section 174. The respondents had failed to do so and were precluded by section 285(1) from taking the point in the Magistrates' Court.

Section 285(1) does not preclude a challenge by way of judicial review questioning the validity of a notice on grounds outside section 174.

Davy v Spelthorne Borough Council (1984)

'If, for example, the respondent had alleged that the enforcement notice had been vitiated by fraud, because one of the appellants' officers had been bribed to issue it, or had been served without the appellants' authority, he would indeed have been questioning its validity, but not on any of the grounds on which an appeal may be brought under [Part VII].' (Lord Fraser of Tullybelton)

Where an enforcement notice complies with the formal requirements of the 1990 Act and has not actually been quashed on appeal or by way of judicial review, then it cannot be challenged in a criminal prosecution.

R v Wicks (Peter Edward) (1997)

The defendant was prosecuted for failing to comply with an enforcement notice. In his defence he sought to challenge the validity of the notice on the basis that the council had acted in bad faith, had been motivated by immaterial considerations and had not genuinely considered whether service of the notice was 'expedient' as required by the 1990 Act.

The House of Lords held that the validity of an enforcement notice which is formally valid and which has not been quashed cannot be challenged by way of a defence to a criminal prosecution. Issues which may be raised by way of judicial review are not suitable for lay justices. Furthermore there has been a consistent statutory policy of restricting the issues that a person prosecuted for non-compliance can raise, so that challenges can be dealt with quickly and enforcement can be effective.

Section 285 does not preclude a defence on the basis that the activities alleged in the notice were not actually taking place at a date after the notice came into effect. The prosecution must still prove its case.

Badcock v Hertfordshire County Council (2002)

Enforcement and stop notices were issued in respect of the importation and processing of waste. The defendant, a building contractor, was prosecuted for non-compliance. He alleged that at the date of the enforcement notice he was not importing and processing waste, but recycling 'surplus building material'.

The Court of Appeal held that it cannot be challenged that, as at the date of the notice, the land was being used for the importing and processing of waste, for to do so would be to raise issues of the validity and enforceability of the notice, which could be raised under ground (b). However, the defendant was not precluded from claiming that at the dates of alleged non-compliance, no waste was actually being imported. The prosecution must prove that the acts of the defendant constituted a breach of the notice.

4.10.5 Penalties

Section 179(8)

'A person guilty of an offence under this section shall be liable:

(a) on summary conviction, to a fine not exceeding £20,000; and

(b) on conviction on indictment, to a fine.'

Section 179(9)

'In determining the amount of any fine to be imposed on a person convicted of an offence under this section, the court shall in particular have regard to any financial benefit which has accrued or appears likely to accrue to him in consequence of the offence.'

Section 179(9) is aimed at developers who profit from unauthorised development. But it does not say that the penalty should be fixed solely by reference to the accrued benefit. Other factors including the seriousness of the offence and the financial circumstances of the offender must be taken into account.

R v Browning (Derek) (1996)

The defendant, without planning permission, erected an outbuilding for stabling his horses at a cost of £80,000. The judge in the Crown Court therefore imposed a fine of £25,000, on the basis that the value of the property had been enhanced by the amount of the outlay.

The Court of Appeal held that the judge had erred in not taking account of the defendant's ability to pay (required by the *Criminal Justice Act* 1991, now the *Criminal Justice Act* 2003). Furthermore, no substantial gain was likely to be achieved provided that planning control was duly enforced and the building demolished. In addition, the judge did not have regard to the expenditure involved in erecting the building. While allowing for the defendant's financial difficulties, a substantial penalty had to be imposed in view of the flagrant breach. The Court substituted a fine of £1,000.

4.10.6   Compliance does not discharge a notice – section 181

Prosser v Sharp (1985)

The Divisional Court held that removing a caravan and replacing it with another does not comply with an enforcement notice requiring the removal of a caravan.

4.10.7   Effect of planning permission on enforcement notice – section 180

An enforcement notice ceases to have effect in so far as it is inconsistent with the subsequent grant of permission. (The same applies to a breach of condition notice, below.) This does not affect liability for previous offences.

R v Chichester Justices, ex parte Chichester District Council (1990)

A two-storey building was required to be removed. The owner did not comply with the enforcement notice but submitted an application for planning permission for a single storey building which was granted. The local authority prosecuted the owner for non-compliance. He claimed that the planning permission terminated the enforcement notice. (The wording of the predecessor to section 180 did not use the phrase 'so far as inconsistent'.)

The Divisional Court held that the enforcement notice only ceases to have effect so far as it is inconsistent with the planning permission. There is no need to demolish the entire building and then build the new one. Parts of the building must be removed so that it becomes the permitted building.

4.11 STOP NOTICES – SECTION 183

Section 183(1)

'Where the local planning authority consider it expedient that any relevant activity should cease before the expiry of the period for compliance with an enforcement notice, they may, when they serve the copy of the enforcement notice or afterwards, serve a notice (in this Act referred to as a "stop notice") prohibiting the carrying out of that activity on the land to which the enforcement notice relates, or any part of that land specified in the stop notice.'

'Relevant activity' is defined in section 183(2) as any activity specified in the enforcement notice that is required to cease. It includes any activity carried out as part of that activity or associated with that activity.

The activity prohibited must be included in a matter alleged by the enforcement notice, or associated with it, to constitute a breach of planning control.

Clwyd County Council v Secretary of State for Wales (1982)

A planning condition required adequate fencing to be constructed before quarrying operations were carried out. No fence was constructed and an enforcement notice was served alleging a failure to fence. The related stop notice could not require a fence to be built (it could only require an activity to cease) so it required the working to cease. (Today a better alternative would be a breach of condition notice.)

The High Court held that the notice was invalid as it was not an activity consisting of or included in any matter alleged to be a breach by the enforcement notice.

Mr Justice Forbes granted the developer's request that the local authority be ordered to withdraw the stop notice (thereby triggering the right to compensation).

4.11.1   Whether 'expedient' – application of government policy

Circular 10/97 states that local planning authorities should ensure that a quick but thorough assessment of the likely consequences of serving a stop notice is available. The assessment should examine the foreseeable costs and benefits likely to result from a stop notice. The stop notice should prohibit only what is essential to safeguard amenity or public safety or prevent serious or irreversible harm to the environment.

The circular is advisory and not binding on the authority if they can show adequate reasons not to follow the advice. In some cases a detailed assessment is not required.

R v Elmbridge Borough Council, ex parte Wendy Fair Markets Ltd (1994)

An inspector had concluded that an area of land was a strategically valuable component of the open corridor along the River Wey and was a weighty justification for green belt designation. Enforcement and stop notices were served in respect of a weekly Sunday market on this land. It was contended that the authority had failed to carry out a proper cost/benefit assessment.

The court held that as there was no activity which was having any serious effect on the amenity of the local residents or environment, the authority were entitled to decide that a cost/benefit assessment was not appropriate. The local authority were familiar with the site and, as a matter of common sense, had realised that the stop notice would effectively prevent the operators and traders from continuing with the Sunday market. Against that the council had to weigh the seriousness of the green belt objection. They had done so and were not required to go into a more detailed economic analysis. It was for the local authority to decide on the expediency of a stop notice and the court should not submit its own view.

Circular 10/97 advises discussions about alternative means of operation where practicable, but there is no legal duty to consult in this way.

R v Hounslow London Borough Council, ex parte Dooley (2000)

On 3 November the local planning authority issued and served copies of an enforcement notice in respect of a restaurant and wine bar and the erection and use of extract ducting at the rear of the property. A stop notice was served on the same day. As the applicants contested the validity of service of the stop notice, a second stop notice was served on 10 November in the same terms as the first. The recipients applied for judicial review of the notices claiming that they should have been consulted first and that there was no power to serve a second notice.

The judge refused the application. Circular 10/97 advises discussions about alternative means of production or operation where practicable, but there is no legal duty to consult in this way. There is a clear danger that, in certain cases, consultation could frustrate the purpose of the stop notice.

There is nothing in the statute to limit the number of notices. The stop notices were consistent and there was no need to choose between the two.

4.11.2 Activities which may not be prohibited

(i)   Use of a building as a dwellinghouse – section 183(3).

(ii)   Any activity which commenced more than four years previously – section 183(4). (This replaces the old

12-month rule.) No account is taken of any period during which the activity was authorised by planning permission (also altering the pre-1991 law). (This exclusion does not apply to activities involved in operational development or deposit of waste – section 183(5A).)

Formal disproof of four years of activity is not a condition precedent to service of a stop notice.

R v Epping Forest District Council, ex parte Strandmill Ltd (1989)

The applicant sought judicial review of the decision of the local authority to issue a stop notice. One of the grounds was that there was evidence that the activity (Sunday markets) had been carried on for more than 12 months [under the previous rule – now four years] and the authority should have established the facts.

Mr Justice Nolan held that it would be unrealistic to suppose that local authorities conduct the equivalent of a trial upon it being known that the 12-month rule is being invoked.

> 'The stop notice is an emergency procedure. Provided that the [local authority] have in mind the drastic character of its effects and provided they approach it in accordance with Wednesbury principles ... their decision should be free from challenge. Subject to this proviso, the interests of the individual harmed by the notice must, under this admittedly hard law, give way to the interests of the community.'

A defendant can defend a prosecution on the ground that the activity has exceeded the time limit.

R v Jenner (1983)

The defendant was prosecuted for failing to comply with a stop notice. He wished to defend himself by establishing that the activities complained of had been commenced more than 12 months before the service of the notice. The trial judge ruled that the stop notice could not be challenged except by way of judicial review and he was convicted.

The Court of Appeal quashed his conviction. The Court observed that judicial review is not suited to resolving issues of fact. The defendant would be liable to criminal penalty and could not defend himself other than by seeking to quash the notice. The defendant was therefore entitled to attempt to establish that he was not prohibited from carrying on his activities by the terms of the prohibition on the face of the stop notice.

4.11.3 The effective date

A stop notice must specify a date when it takes effect, not earlier than three days after the date when the notice is served, unless there are special reasons and a statement of those reasons is served with the stop notice. The date the notice takes effect must not be later than 28 days from the date when the notice was first served on any person.

R v Hounslow London Borough Council, ex parte Dooley (2000)

A notice served on 3 November was expressed to take effect on 6 November. The applicants contended that the day of service should be excluded in calculating the period, and so the notice should have been expressed to take effect no earlier than 7 November. The judge preferred the clear words of the statute. Three days after 3 November is 6 November.

4.11.4 Service of notice

As with all statutory notices, this is governed by section 329 which provides for various modes of service. See the *Dooley* case below.

4.11.5 Offence – section 187

A person who contravenes a stop notice after a site notice has been displayed or the stop notice has been served on him is guilty of an offence. Contravening includes causing or permitting contravention – section 187(1B). (See *Ragsdale v Creswick*, 4.10.3, as to permitting.)

Section 187(3) defence

It is a defence for the accused to prove that the stop notice was not served on him and that he did not know, and could not reasonably have been expected to know, of its existence.

It was claimed in the *Dooley* case that the effect of section 187(3) is that notice must be served on the defendant in person. The court dismissed this.

R v Hounslow London Borough Council, ex parte Dooley (2000)

The judge held that section 187(3) carries no implication that the service of a stop notice is to be by personal delivery. Service is governed by section 329, which provides for various modes of service for any notice served under the 1990 Act. Furthermore, the effect of the provision is that, provided the notice has been served on one person who appears to have an interest in the land or to be engaged in any prohibited activity (section 183(6)), *any* person may be guilty of contravening it after a site notice has been displayed, unless he has no actual or constructive knowledge of its existence.

Penalties – section 187(2), (2A)

These are the same as for enforcement notices – see 4.10.5.

4.11.6 Compensation for loss due to stop notice – section 186

Compensation is due if the enforcement notice is quashed on any grounds other than appeal ground (a) – that permission should be granted or a condition discharged.

Compensation is due if the enforcement notice is varied (other than on ground (a)) so that any activity prohibited by the stop notice ceases to be a relevant activity.

Compensation is due if the enforcement notice is withdrawn by the local planning authority otherwise than in consequence of the grant of permission.

Compensation is due if the stop notice is withdrawn.

Where the enforcement notice or stop notice is a nullity there can be no compensation. But the court may order the authority to withdraw the notice.

Clwyd County Council v Secretary of State for Wales (1982)

The stop notice was held to be 'hopelessly invalid'. Mr Justice Forbes stated that if he made the order asked for, namely that Clwyd should withdraw the notice, the way was open for the developer to claim compensation. This would preclude their claim for damages.

Amount of compensation

Compensation is payable in respect of any loss or damage directly attributable to the stop notice prohibition and is not linked to depreciation in land value. Disputes are settled by the Lands Tribunal.

Robert Barnes & Co v Malvern Hills District Council (1985)

The planning authority served enforcement and stop notices in respect of house building in the belief that the relevant planning permission had expired. The enforcement notice was quashed on the ground that the matters alleged in the notice did not constitute a breach. RB & Co sought compensation in the region of £500,000, a large proportion of which was based on the claim that capital was tied up in the site, which was locked up and could not be worked.

The Lands Tribunal accepted the authority's case that the stop notice came at a time when there was a serious recession in the business of residential development and that, even without the stop notice, it would have been in the interest of the company to delay work on the subject land until market conditions improved. A sum of £82,000 was awarded for interest on land acquisition costs, abortive expenditure, professional fees, and losses on a bungalow which became semi-derelict when the site was abandoned.

4.11.7 Challenging a stop notice

There is no right of appeal against a stop notice. However, the validity of a stop notice can be challenged by way of judicial review. Furthermore in *R v Jenner* (above) expiry of the time limit can be used as a defence in a criminal court.

Likewise, matters concerning the factual basis of the stop notice can be raised by way of defence and are not precluded by section 285(1) (see 4.10.4) which only applies to enforcement notices.

Badcock v Hertfordshire County Council (2002)

The defendant alleged that at the date of the enforcement notice the matters alleged had not occurred. The Court of Appeal held that section 285(1) prevented this being raised as a defence to the enforcement notice, since it could have been raised by way of appeal under section 174(2) ground (b). However, the Court held that section 285(1) does not apply to stop notices, even though they are parasitic on enforcement notices. So the question of whether the matters alleged were occurring at the date of the notice could be raised as a defence to the charges in respect of the stop notice.

Stop notice alleged to be excessive

It is admissible to use wording in both enforcement notices and stop notices, which incorporates matters of fact and degree. The recipient must then make a judgment as to whether he is complying with the notices or not.

R v Runnymede Borough Council, ex parte Sarvan Singh (1987)

The applicant, a Sikh, engaged in a variety of religious observances at his home involving many visiting Sikhs. The local planning authority served an enforcement notice requiring the religious purposes, other than those incidental to the enjoyment of the dwellinghouse, to cease. A stop notice was also served.

The applicant was concerned that normal Sikh religious activities of prayer meetings and chanting might be prevented, and sought judicial review claiming that the stop notice was invalid or void in that it did not indicate precisely what he was prohibited from doing.

Mr Justice Schiemann, whilst recognising that the applicant's worries were well founded, said that it was admissible to use wording in both enforcement and stop notices that incorporated matters of fact and degree. The applicant is then left with making a judgment on how to behave. If it is the wrong judgment, he may be punished by the magistrates. Alternatively, he might sail so carefully that he was being deprived of something which he would be entitled to do. Despite this, the notices were valid.

4.12 THE TEMPORARY STOP NOTICE – SECTIONS 171E–H

The *Planning and Compulsory Purchase Act* 2004 creates a new enforcement power, the temporary stop notice. Such a notice stops activity immediately without having to issue an enforcement notice. See the *Town and Country Planning (Temporary Stop Notice) (England) Regulations* 2005 and Circular 02/05.

4.13 THE PLANNING CONTRAVENTION NOTICE – SECTION 171C

Section 171C(1)

'Where it appears to the local planning authority that there may have been a breach of planning control in respect of any land, they may serve notice to that effect ... on any person who:

(a)   is the owner or occupier of the land or has any other interest in it; or

(b)   is carrying out any operations on the land or using it for any purpose.'

In short, the planning contravention notice requires the recipient to provide information about what uses, operations or activities are taking place on the land and who is or may be responsible. Improper failure to reply within 21 days is an offence.

It must 'appear' to the authority that there 'may' have been a breach. The validity of a notice may be challenged by way of judicial review.

R v Teignbridge District Council, ex parte Teignmouth Quay Co Ltd (1995)

The Teignmouth Quay Co began work on a new building. The company assured the planning authority that the building was for use in connection with the handling of cargoes and so was permitted development under the GDO. Local opposition resulted in the local authority serving a planning contravention notice. The company applied to the High Court for judicial review of the decision to serve the notice.

Mr Justice Judge quashed the decision to serve the notice. It must appear to the authority that there may have been a breach. Service is not justified because it appears to someone else that there may be a breach. There was nothing to suggest the slightest suspicion of a possible breach of planning control. No reasonable planning authority could have concluded that it appeared there may have been a breach.

4.14 THE BREACH OF CONDITION NOTICE – SECTION 187A

Enforcement action is the issuing of an enforcement notice or the service of a breach of condition notice – section 171A(2).

No enforcement action in respect of a breach of condition may be taken after the end of the period of ten years beginning with the date of breach (see *Dilieto v Ealing London Borough Council*, at 4.14.1) unless an enforcement notice is in effect – section 171B(3).

Section 187A(2)

If a planning condition has not been complied with, the local planning authority may serve a breach of condition notice on:

(a) any person who is carrying out or who has carried out the development; or

(b) any person having control of the land,

requiring him to secure compliance with such of the conditions as are specified in the notice.

Section 187A(5)

'A breach of condition notice shall specify the steps which the authority consider ought to be taken or the activities which the authority consider ought to cease, to secure compliance with the conditions specified in the notice.'

The steps must be very clearly specified so that the recipient knows exactly what he is required to do.

R v East Lothian Council, ex parte Scottish Coal Co Ltd (2001)

Planning permission for an open cast coal site was granted subject to various conditions. One of the conditions required the operator, in the event of a complaint about noise, to immediately notify the planning authority and undertake an investigation in consultation with the planning authority and initiate any necessary remedial measures.

A breach of condition notice was served in respect of this condition. The notice stated that the operator was to:

- ensure that an investigation is undertaken in consultation with the Council and that any necessary remedial measures agreed with the Council are initiated; and
- ensure that in the event of further complaint an investigation is undertaken in consultation with the council.

It was held that the notice was not valid as it did not 'specify' actual steps but simply echoed the condition. Thus the operator had no notice of what was expected in practical terms and so no way of knowing whether or not any particular course of action would constitute failure to take steps and be a criminal offence. To 'ensure' focuses on the result to be achieved rather than the means of achieving it.

If the steps specified in the notice are not taken within the period allowed for compliance in the notice (at least 28 days) the 'person responsible' (the person on whom the notice is served) is guilty of an offence.

4.14.1 Challenging the breach of condition notice

Section 73 application

There is no right to appeal against a breach of condition notice, but an application may be made under section 73 for the release of the condition (see 3.4.5).

Judicial review

The validity of a breach of condition notice may be challenged by way of judicial review in the High Court.

A notice may be quashed for error of law if there is no breach of condition.

R v Ealing London Borough Council, ex parte Zainuddain (1995)

Planning permission was granted for the erection of a mosque on condition that no religious or ceremonial buildings or acts of worship could take place within the site except within the building, and no part of the development could be occupied until the buildings were satisfactorily completed. The site was cleared and a foundation ceremony was attended by 500 people. £30,000 was spent on scaffolding and corrugated sheeting to completely envelop the gathering. The planning authority served a breach of condition notice complaining that both conditions had been broken.

The High Court quashed the notice. There was no breach of either condition. First, the structure could properly be described as a building, although not roofed. Second, occupied meant 'starting to use on a settled basis'.

Defence to a prosecution

As there is no right of appeal against a breach of condition notice, the courts have held that the defendant may challenge its validity in prosecution proceedings (unlike enforcement notices – see 4.10.4). This may extend to challenging the lawfulness of the condition itself, however, questions of *Wednesbury* unreasonableness, improper motive or irrelevant considerations should be dealt with by way of judicial review.

Dilieto v Ealing London Borough Council (1998)

Planning permission was granted in 1964 for a warehouse subject to a condition that a yard area 'be maintained clear at all times to the satisfaction of the local planning authority'. In 1994 the council found that the yard was being used for the parking and storage of ice-cream vans. In 1995 a breach of condition notice was served and the appellant was prosecuted. The appellant claimed that the notice was out of time and that the condition was void for uncertainty, but the magistrates held that the validity of the notice could not be challenged in criminal proceedings.

The Divisional Court held that the defendant could challenge the notice on the basis that it was out of time, because under section 171B 'enforcement action' cannot be taken after the expiry of the time limit. The defendant would have to prove ten years' use according to the civil standard of proof.

The Court went further and stated that a notice could also be challenged on the ground that the relevant condition was so vague and imprecise as to be a nullity. Given that there was no right of appeal against a breach of condition notice, it would need very clear words to exclude a challenge to the lawfulness of the condition. Nevertheless, there is a limit to the scope of challenge in criminal proceedings, and it would normally be inappropriate to raise questions of *Wednesbury* unreasonableness before magistrates.

(The notice was held to be sufficiently certain.)

4.15 INJUNCTIONS – SECTION 187B

Section 187B(1)

'Where a local planning authority consider it necessary or expedient for any actual or apprehended breach of planning control to be restrained by injunction, they may apply to the court for an injunction, whether or not they have exercised or are proposing to exercise any of their other powers under this Part.'

The court may commit to prison a person in breach of an injunction.

The court has a broad discretion when considering whether to grant the remedy of an injunction. Although the judge must take the planning merits as decided within the planning process, he must take into account the personal circumstances of the defendant in accordance with the principle of proportionality. Any interference with a right within the

European Convention on Human Rights must be proportionate to the intended objective. It must not be arbitrary or unfair.

South Buckinghamshire District Council v Porter; Chichester District Council v Searle; Wrexham County Borough Council v Berry; Hertsmere Borough Council v Hatty (2003)

These cases concerned gypsies who had failed to obtain planning permission for sites that they owned. Injunctions had been granted but overturned by the Court of Appeal. The local authorities appealed.

The House of Lords upheld the guidance given in the Court of Appeal in the leading judgment of Lord Justice Simon Brown in the light of the *Human Rights Act* 1998. In short, the judge must accept that the planning merits have been decided but he should not grant an injunction unless he would be prepared to send the defendant to prison for breach. He would not be of this mind unless he had considered all questions of hardship for the defendant and his family including health and education, and the availability of alternative sites. He must also consider countervailing matters such as flagrancy of breach, the need to enforce planning control in the general interest and the planning history of the site.

As to proportionality, Lord Justice Simon Brown said:

'Proportionality requires not only that the injunction be appropriate and necessary for the attainment of the public interest objective sought – here the safeguarding of the environment – but also that it does not impose an excessive burden on the individual whose private interest – here the gipsy's private life and home and the retention of his ethnic identity – are at stake.'

Matters which could be raised in an enforcement notice appeal cannot be raised in injunction proceedings – *North West Estates plc v Buckinghamshire County Council* (2003).

Index

The *Case in Point* series

The *Case in Point* series is a popular set of concise practical guides to legal issues in land, property and construction. Written for the property professional, they get straight to the key issues in a refreshingly jargon-free style.

Areas covered:

Negligence in Valuation and Surveys
Stock code: 6388
Published: December 2002

Party Walls
Stock code: 7269
Published: May 2004

Service Charges
Stock code: 7272
Published: June 2004

Estate Agency
Stock code: 7472
Published: July 2004

Rent Review
Stock code: 8531
Published: May 2005

Expert Witness
Stock code: 8842
Published: August 2005

Lease Renewal
Stock code: 8711
Published: August 2005

VAT in Property and Construction
Stock code: 8840
Published September 2005

Construction Adjudication
Stock code: 9040
Published October 2005

Dilapidations
Stock code: 9113
Published January 2006

If you would like to be kept informed when new *Case in Point* titles are published, please e-mail **rbmarketing@rics.org.uk**

All RICS Books titles can be ordered direct by:

☎ Telephoning 0870 333 1600 (Option 3)

🖰 Online at www.ricsbooks.com

🖷 E-mail mailorder@rics.org.uk